Praise for *Supply Chains to Virtual Integration*

"Building viable e-businesses requires that companies separate real trends from the overabundant e-hype. In this quest, the old quote, "The devil is in the details," is particularly apropos. Ram Reddy's book is a tour-de-force in integrating both a broad vision of supply chain management with the often-missing nuance and detail required to successfully implement it."

—Jim Highsmith, Director, E-Project Management Practice,
Cutter Consortium, and author of *Adaptive Software Development:
A Collaborative Approach to Managing Complex Systems*

"*Supply Chains to Virtual Integration* is the definitive book on how traditional supply chain management is shifting to a more sophisticated discipline. The authors wisely emphasize organizational, business process, and technical infrastructure alignment as key factors in this transition. Their chapter on virtual integration conveys how the modern enterprise can thrive as traditional corporate boundaries fade away. This is a must-read for managers and executives engaged in supply chain management."

—William M. Ulrich, President,
Tactical Strategy Group, Inc.

"This book provides a unique framework for addressing a wide variety of critical business issues related to the management of information technology. Many valuable insights are derived from a very thorough analysis of factors affecting the net benefits of technology. The authors describe these factors from within the context of supply chains and trading networks. This integrative approach is a most-welcomed addition to the literature."

—Peter A. Silhan, Associate Professor, Information Systems,
College of Commerce and Business Administration,
University of Illinois at Urbana-Champaign

"Companies often view e-commerce, supply chain management, technology, and process reengineering as separate and disparate initiatives. *Supply Chains to Virtual Integration* provides a definitive roadmap for managing these not as disparate initiatives but as a fluid and integrated program for continuous improvement. Its unique blend of management theory and substantive guidance make this a must-read for modern change agents."

—David Vasile, Vice President/General Manager,
Handleman Online

"Supply Chains to Virtual Integration provides an excellent framework for the examination of supply chain issues from an organizational behavior perspective. Their methodology of a rapid but incremental approach to supply chain management technology integration focuses on one of the most important IT issues today; that being the organizational change management required for successful implementation of new business systems."

—Adolph T. Barclift Jr., Senior Vice President,
Business Development, Knowledge Decision Sciences, Inc.

Emerging Business Technology Series

SUPPLY CHAINS TO VIRTUAL INTEGRATION

**Ram Reddy and
Sabine Reddy, Ph.D.**

McGraw-Hill

New York   Chicago   San Francisco   Lisbon   London
Madrid   Mexico City   Milan   New Delhi   San Juan
Seoul   Singapore   Sydney   Toronto

Library of Congress Cataloging-in-Publication Data

Reddy, Ram.
    Supply chains to virtual integration/ by Ram Reddy & Sabine Reddy.
       p. cm. — (Emerging business technology series)
    Includes bibliographical references.
    ISBN 0-07-137465-5
    1. Business logistics. I. Sabine, Reddy. II. Title. III. Series.
HD38.5 .R43 2001
658.5—dc21   2001030893

McGraw-Hill

A Division of The McGraw·Hill Companies

1 2 3 4 5 6 7 8 9 0 AGM/AGM 0 9 8 7 6 5 4 3 2 1

ISBN 0-07-137465-5

*This book was set in Sabon by MM Design 2000, Inc.
Printed and bound by Quebecor World/Martinsburg.*

Many thanks to Nancy Warner for her development work on this book.

McGraw-Hill books are available at special quantity discounts to use as premiums
and sales promotions, or for use in corporate training programs. For more information, please write to the Director of Special Sales, Professional Publishing, McGraw-
Hill, Two Penn Plaza, New York, NY 10121-2298. Or contact your local bookstore.

 This book is printed on recycled, acid-free paper containing a minimum of
50% recycled, de-inked fiber.

To our mentors and teachers

who have shared their knowledge

and helped us succeed in our professions.

Contents

Foreword

Today, we stand at a crossroads: The scale and scope of interenterprise relationships is an economic revolution reshaping the face of business. As competition intensifies, and as pressure to cut costs and boost efficiencies increases, the structure of interenterprise relationships is undergoing radical transformation.

To understand where we are headed, it is important to understand where we came from. At the turn of the last century, a typical manufacturing firm owned all activities related to the upstream acquisition and conversion of raw materials into finished goods. More often than not, the same firm delivered the final product downstream to the consumer. For example, Ford Motor Company owned the mines, power plants, steel mills, and other sources of raw materials required to produce Model T cars. Ford was a fully integrated conglomerate—a tight collection of closely related business units.

The industrial era was characterized by significant economies of scale and mass production. A major advantage and disadvantage of this organizational model was the high fixed costs that companies had to bear in order to compete. These high fixed costs restricted the amount of resources a firm could invest in new products, which did not use materials from the current raw material supply chain.

Over time, these vertically integrated industrial firms realized that they needed to limit their focus to their core competencies and specialties. This decision drastically changed corporate architecture and helped reduce operating costs and capital spending, improved asset utilization, and increased speed-to-market. As a result, the corporate architecture of large companies separated into multiple models that often operated under the same roof. Some of these operating models included outsourcing, mergers and acquisitions, and either internal startups or stand-alone "e" companies. These new models were essential to provide strategic flexibility.

Few executives would deny that their industries are undergoing a radical transformation. For example, the semiconductor and high-tech industries have adopted the outsourcing model with a vengeance. Using partners to complement the manufacturing needs of original equipment manufacturers (OEMs), such as Nokia or Motorola, is a thriving industry. As OEMs outsource more services, a growing number of companies—Solectron and Flextronics—are creating one-stop shops to reduce time-to-market and time-to-volume pressures while simultaneously lowering costs and increasing flexibility. The range of services provided by these companies includes design, manufacturing, assembly, and aftermarket repair services. OEMs are changing the nature of strategic cross-enterprise partnerships by seeking suppliers capable of not only providing product but also high-quality process skills coupled with engineering and design know-how.

The economic and technological forces shaping the high-tech industry are bearing down on industries everywhere. The old adage "It's what's inside that counts" no longer dominates strategy. The realization that "core competencies" are not rigid or fixed is starting to set in. Connecting to what's outside efficiently and effectively is what matters in today's business environment in which demands of greater speed of service, flexibility, and resources are beyond what any single company can provide.

New virtual integration solutions are required for companies seeking to link their alliances, outsourcing partners, M&A, and dot.com channels. Market observers have labeled this trend by a variety of different names: business webs, coalitions, extended enterprises, borderless corporations, value nets, keiretsu, joint ventures, consortia, and connected corporations.

The terminology may be different, but the gospel is the same: Successful companies must be positioned to operate in a multiorganizational network with the flexibility to quickly apply capital and talent to those opportunities with the greatest potential for maximizing shareholder value. This new model is a complex mixture of the traditional business hierarchy—characterized by centralized control—and market models where control is decentralized or nonexistent.

Yet, despite this outpouring of breakthrough thinking, prescriptions, and diagnoses, not much has been implemented. A number of companies have taken the first steps to address the structural problems that have been accumulating for many years, and some have made considerable progress. However, too few have fully grasped and implemented the kind of fundamental changes that the new virtual economy requires, changes that usually begin with the customer-facing process but extend to encompass the entire supply chain.

Gradually but relentlessly, the structural migration from vertical integration to virtual integration is taking place in the economy. Why haven't more firms responded to the virtual integration vision? How should they respond? What approaches have proven to be successful? How do we overcome the gap between vision and implementation? In the pages that follow Ram Reddy and Sabine Reddy provide answers that are critical for every firm. Make no mistake; every firm is dealing with virtual integration issues.

Is your firm ready?

Ravi Kalakota
CEO, E-BusinessStrategies

Preface

Making the Transition

The old Chinese proverb "May you live in interesting times" has special meaning for managers working in major corporations around the world. Constant change, propelled by information technologies (IT), is making the job of managers increasingly difficult. Product life cycles are getting shorter; barriers to entry are falling; globalization is changing the entire competitive landscape in certain industries. At the same time, there is constant pressure on management from stakeholders to deliver increasing value—financial quarter after quarter. Mergers and acquisitions and corporate divestitures are changing the way firms work—internally, with their suppliers, and with their customers.

As the window of opportunity to realize the benefits from an innovative product or concept gets smaller and smaller, a firm's competitive agility has become critical. Given this turbulent environment, some management gurus question the need for long-term strategy and recommend planning for uncertainty instead. Many firms have already developed a vision of how to transform their businesses so that they can function in the electronic business arena. Unfortunately, translating the visions to actionable plans is a difficult proposition.

We are told that revolutionary information technologies are radically redefining the way firms do business. The term "revolution" implies the necessity of a quick response, which makes the transition challenging because IT innovations impact all areas of a firm. Given the potential benefit, across all areas of a firm, of using IT technologies to increase competitive advantage, most managers feel like a deer caught in the headlights—frozen and unable to move or decide where to begin the transformation process and which technology to use.

Based on the infrastructure provided by Internet technologies, we believe that there are fundamental changes occurring in the way firms design, assemble, deliver, and support products and services. However, this is a process of evolution, not revolution. Our book presents a framework with which managers can help transition their firm and its supporting supply chain to pursue strategic business objectives while retaining competitive agility.

"The more things change. . ."

To quote noted economists Carl Shapiro and Hal Varian from their book *Information Rules*:

> [D]urable economic principles can guide you in today's frenetic business environment. Technology changes. Economic laws do not.[1]

Our approach to the Web-based technological evolution is based on sound economic and management principles that have been proven over time. We present a framework that enables managers to identify areas of value within the firm and across the supply chain that can be mined using Internet technologies. The opportunities highlighted in this book existed even before the advent of Internet technologies. Firms have long attempted to use IT to make their operations more efficient and effective. However, no previous technology provided the same degree of flexibility and open architecture as the Web-based technologies. Competitive flexibility was difficult to achieve with proprietary information technologies.

This opportunity for flexibility has important implications for the organizational structures and processes within firms. We argue that technology in and of itself can't add value without simultaneously changing the firm's

---

[1] C. Shapiro and H. R. Varian, *Information Rules*, Harvard Business School Press, Boston, 1998, pp. 1–2.

supporting processes and structures. Open-architecture technology has freed firms from having to invest in specialized organizational forms and organizational functions that do not directly support firms' primary product or service. Firms can now develop laserlike focus and specialize in a few areas, divesting themselves of functions that are not core to their vision and mission. Ultimately, firms will be able to join forces and disband at will, virtually enabled by information technology.

What This Book Is About

We want to reach managers in all functional areas of a firm: marketing, human resources, finance, manufacturing, purchasing, etc. Because the organizational change associated with implementing the new information technologies affects all these different functional areas, we address many different areas of operations within a firm and across its supply chain. We give specific examples of where a firm can leverage technology, structure, and processes to improve efficiency or enhance competitive flexibility. Although the book provides valuable technical and economic insights for entrepreneurs, we primarily target managers from mature firms to help them transition their legacy systems, processes, and structures to support the need for competitive agility.

Prior to the advent of Internet technologies most firms produced their goods based on forecasted demands. Supply chain systems focused on maximum inventory turns at minimal cost. The overriding objective was efficient utilization of property, plant, equipment, and direct labor. Supply chain systems to accomplish this were based on command and control principles to synchronize the activities of the trading partners in the supply chain. Producing products or services to forecasted demand can also be viewed as "pushing" these products and services through the supply chain and on to the customer.

Facilitated by a variety of Internet technologies, today's consumer can configure and order highly customized products. Here the customers "pull" a product from the supply chain based on their individual tastes. The supply chain has to provide maximum flexibility to support this "build to order" demand. While operational efficiencies do matter, there is a trade-off between customization and the costs of customization. Firms must focus on customer satisfaction, retention, and enhancement.

The supply chain systems supporting forecasted demand models are very different from the supply chain systems supporting customization models. To make matters worse, due to the fact that products shift between the push model and the pull model as they advance through the product life cycle, firms face considerable uncertainty regarding the optimal operational model. A review of these two models will prepare managers to deal with their supply chains and with questions of outsourcing and vertical integration. We will provide a business framework to help managers make their technology choices in the supply chain area.

This book is not meant to be a technical exposition of supply chain principles and systems. However, we will present enough material to help nontechnical managers understand some of the fundamental principles of supply chain management. Most importantly, we want to emphasize how technology will cause the natural evolution of the term *supply chain* beyond the purchasing function into all other business areas within the firm.

Information technology topics are presented to enable the nontechnical manager or executive to make informed IT and architecture decisions. We maintain that the IT function in firms should be to facilitate the technology selection process; managers or executives who understand the long-term implication of the technology choices on a firm's strategic business options must make the actual choice.

Why Should You Read This Book?

This book will provide managers and executives from all functional areas with the necessary background to make informed decisions as their firm enters the era of electronic business. Managers from established firms with legacy systems will learn how to transition their firms to benefit from technology investments in the supply chain area. They will learn to identify the organizational and process changes that are necessary to successfully implement these technologies. Executives will discover the appropriate technology and architecture choices that will allow their firms to shift focus to customer needs and at the same time reduce the constraints imposed by historical investments in physical plant, organization, process, and technology. Executives of "young" firms will learn how to organize for maximum scalability in order to support unexpected increases in demand. Many start-ups with promising product launches fail to make the transition to long-term viability. Our framework will help start-ups better understand the organizational and systems requirements for profitable rapid growth.

The current spate of technology innovations has unleashed a "modern" gold rush. Drawing parallels with the California gold rush, very few firms will find huge gold nuggets lying around. The gold was ultimately collected by sifting through tons of river sediment. Similarly, there are many large pockets of hidden gold dust, or avoidable costs, within firms and across their supply chains. Managers can mine this gold by patiently sifting through departmental processes, organizational structures, and technologies. This book provides the necessary tools for managers to find and eliminate some of the hidden and avoidable costs. Along the way, managers have the added benefit of gradually architecting their firm for competitive agility.

Ram Reddy and Sabine Reddy, April 2001.

Supply Chain Systems and the Network Economy

At the turn of the last century, a typical manufacturing firm owned all production stages of acquiring and converting raw material into a finished product. More often than not, these firms delivered the finished product directly to the consumer. Consider the example of tire manufacturers. A typical company owned rubber plantations in the tropics and facilities to convert rubber sap for use in the tire factories. The manufacturer also owned ships, overland transportation, and warehouses at the docks, ensuring an uninterrupted supply of rubber to factories in Europe and North America. The tires were sold after manufacture through company-owned and -operated outlets. Similarly, automotive manufacturers owned mines, power plants, steel mills, and other raw materials sources needed to produce their final products. The tire and automotive firms described above are examples of vertically integrated firms. The firms' range of activities extended upstream into sources of supply and downstream into selling to customers in company-owned stores.

A major disadvantage of this approach was the high cost of investments a vertically integrated firm had to make in a particular industry. This restricted the resources such a firm could invest in developing new products, which were not based on the supply of current raw materials. Our tire manufacturer, for example, would have to manage the rubber plantation and labor, the shipping firms, captive power plants, and other upstream activities not directly related to the manufacture of tires. This diverted attention from the primary objective of designing and manufacturing tires efficiently. Over time, most vertically integrated firms divested themselves of noncritical upstream and downstream activities. An automotive manufacturer that needed guaranteed access to raw materials could use other methods—such as metal futures markets. Shipping, warehousing, and overland transportation services were bought as needed from firms specializing in these activities. These upstream sources of supply to the manufacturer became the supply chain. The dealers and distributors that replaced the downstream factory-owned stores became the distribution channels and also part of the supply chain.

Firms retained upstream and downstream activities that were critical to ensuring a smooth flow of products to their customers. Their focus, however, shifted to manufacturing their core products efficiently. This era—the industrial age—was characterized by mass production and economies of scale. Information technologies were designed to coordinate the smooth flow of goods and services across the supply chain. The focus was on reducing costs across the supply chain and within the firm. If we are to believe the pundits and many respected economists, business enterprises are in the initial stages of a third evolutionary phase, just as important as the one that led us to the industrial age. The current evolution to the network economy is driven by information technologies, mainly the Internet.

Despite the initial hype and current disillusionment with Internet technologies, the reality is that this evolution is going to continue to develop gradually over the next decade. In trying to sort out media-generated hype from reality, life has become very difficult for managers of so-called bricks-and-mortar firms. Exacerbating the situation is the explosion of new software products and services that claim to make the transition to the network economy easy for firms. Frequent mergers and acquisitions among the technology vendors, and new standards dictated by online marketplaces and trade exchanges, further muddy the technology-selection waters.

Information technology was first introduced into firms through the use of time-sharing mainframe systems. These systems were designed to automate simple repetitive tasks within the firm, improving efficiency and accuracy. The automated tasks were primarily from financial and manufacturing areas such as payroll, billing, and manufacturing resource planning. Only a few specialized functions within the firm had access to information technology. Mainframe technologies were supplanted by client/server technologies that opened the information technology floodgates to every function within the firm. The availability of cheap personal computers coupled with the rapid installation of local- and wide-area networks meant that soon there was a PC on every desk. The significant benefits that accrued from these information technologies were mainly due to increased operating efficiencies and reduced transaction costs, although technology also enabled business-processes reengineering to cut the costs of internal operations.

Most of these technologies—the PC, local area networks, client/server platforms—went through an initial phase of inflated expectations followed by a period of disillusionment before they could be used for productive purposes. Internet technologies that allowed disparate mainframe and client/server systems across multiple firms to talk to one another were hyped not only in the technology but in the popular press as well. They were supposed to revolutionize the way firms conducted their business. The focus shifted from business strategy to Internet business models. The reality is that firms that use Internet technologies to complement their traditional business practices will be able to find sustainable competitive advantages. Unlike previous information technologies that focused on operational efficiencies, Internet technologies have the ability to impact the fundamental structure of a firm and its supply chain. Regardless of the uncertainty and doubt regarding technology choices, information technology is fundamentally changing the way a firm develops, markets, and supports its products and services.

The Web environment has generated opportunities for high-flying Internet firms that have been frequently covered in the popular press. However, Web technologies also generate new opportunities for traditional bricks-and-mortar firms, which can achieve significant cost reductions and operational effectiveness by redefining business processes in the supply chain and distribution networks. It is important to understand that many of these tangible benefits can be realized quickly and with modest investments in the right technologies.

There have been numerous books written—and many more will be written—highlighting the strategic requirements to succeed in the "new economy" or the "knowledge economy." Similarly, there are technical books dealing with all aspects of Internet technologies, from new programming environments to universal communications standards. However, these efforts, while laudable, remain rather disjointed, and do not offer implementation guidelines derived from the strategic choices. In this new network economy, with its technological options, the business strategy of a firm will be dramatically affected by the technology choices it makes. Therefore it is important for managers both from general business and from information technology (IT) areas to understand the technology drivers for the economy, their industry, and their firm.

Using an organizational process and IT perspective, we will discuss how strategic business drivers map to tactical initiatives. We will also discuss the impact of technology choices on business strategy. It is our contention that significant technological and economic changes within individual enterprises and across the supply chain are going to occur over the next decade. During this important transition period, managers and executives will have to keep making technology, process, and organizational choices as they relate to their particular product or service. This book is aimed at helping executives, line managers, and IT managers make informed technology and process decisions that are appropriate for their particular product or service today, but also allow competitive flexibility for the future.

Evolution of the Business Enterprise

It is important to understand the strategic and economic changes occurring in the economy as a whole and within specific business enterprises. The technology selections that a manager makes should not only address current problems faced by the firm, but also create the infrastructure that will allow future competitive flexibility. The adage "The only constant is change" is truly reflective of our era, and all technology decisions have to factor this into the decision-making process.

The first major evolution of the business enterprise occurred after the American Civil War. During this evolution, the concept of ownership was separated from management. Professional managers were hired to run hitherto family-owned enterprises, after many prominent firms of that period were run into the ground by successive generations of ever-more-incompetent members of the founding families.

The professional managerial era set the stage for the second evolution of the business enterprise, which was characterized by the emergence of mass production. The entire firm was organized for command and control of the firm's resources to achieve economies of scale. The organizational structure and resulting information systems were geared to support functional and operational efficiencies. Alfred Sloan's redesign of General Motors and General Electric's massive restructuring of the 1950s characterize the peak of the second stage of the evolution of the business enterprise. Information systems from that era and all subsequent computerized systems focused mainly on achieving operational efficiencies and control over functional areas. Processes and technology were primarily driven by the requirements of mass production.

Over the past few years, Fortune 500–type firms have reengineered their internal processes and systems using technologies such as enterprise resource planning (ERP) systems. Where implemented correctly, these systems have provided significant advantages in operational effectiveness and profitability. Just like their predecessors, these systems are inward-looking and focus on efficiency. They are sophisticated and refined descendants of the second evolution. Using ever more advanced statistical and operations research tools, firms have continued to organize their resources to push products efficiently to their customers while trying to match forecasted market demand. Technology-enabled supply chain systems have led to tight vertical process integration and better utilization of fixed assets and working capital. Just-in-time (JIT) systems have become the symbol of tightly integrated supply chain systems. The term *market economy model* describes the vertically integrated firm of the second evolutionary stage that "pushes" product to the customer based on forecasted market demand. An example of a firm following this model is a car manufacturer. The investments in property, plant, and equipment needed to manufacture an automobile are huge and require efficient management. For optimal and full utilization of a manufacturing shift, cars are manufactured to match predicted demand.

The third evolution of the business enterprise has been fueled by information systems and accelerated by Internet technologies that have allowed disparate information systems to interact with one another. Internet technologies have led to the rapid emergence of business networks within and outside the firm to satisfy the strategic desire for competitive flexibility. As opposed to the market economy model, where firms "push" product to the customer based on forecasts, the network economy model is geared toward the customer "pulling" products customized to his or her individual needs. In the network economy model of the third evolution, the firm's resources are organized to meet the unpredictable demand patterns of the customer.

An example of a firm following the pull model is a supplier of content for readers of digital books. Once the reader pays the fee to read a book, the publisher downloads the book to whatever device the reader is using. There are hardly any manufacturing or storage costs associated with the digital content. Here the consumer "pulls" highly customized digital content to his or her reader as needed. It follows that the supply chain systems to support the network economy and market economy models are very different, as illustrated in Figure 1.1.

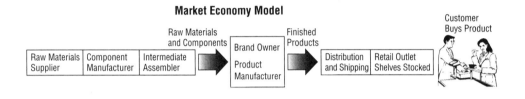

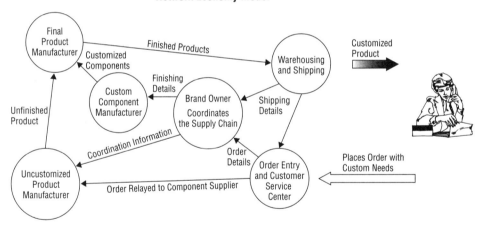

Figure 1.1: A comparison of market economy and network economy models.

Transition in Supply Chain Management: From Efficiency to Flexibility

Reengineering efforts over the past few years have been inwardly focused, directed toward removing internal operating inefficiencies and unnecessary costs from within the enterprise. More recently, the focus of cost reductions has shifted outside the firm to costs of procuring commodity items and operating materials that are not part of the standard market economy supply chain solutions.

A typical manufacturing enterprise spends approximately 57 percent of its revenue on outside purchase of goods and services. These purchases fall into four broad categories:

- Capital expenditures
- Low-value nonrecurring purchases
- High-value, high-volume strategic raw materials
- Low-value, high-volume maintenance, repair, and operations (MRO) materials for commodity items

High-value, high-volume strategic raw materials already are procured through tightly integrated technology-enabled supply chains. By leveraging IT solutions to simplify business processes, considerable additional cost savings and operational efficiencies can be achieved in the MRO and commodity procurement areas.

Enabled by technology, loosely coupled networks of suppliers, manufacturers, and external service providers develop innovative and customized products. In such a system, the customer is exposed to product specification, ordering, and other processes within the enterprise, changing the traditional methods of customer interaction. Customer involvement has resulted in increased customer satisfaction and reduced transaction costs. As the network economy model evolves, more sophisticated and pervasive information technology will change the definition of a traditional supply chain to include customers, service providers, and outsourcers.

Long a strategic imperative proposed by management experts, adopting the network economy model allows firms to drive fixed-asset costs out by subcontracting nonstrategic tasks and focusing on core competencies. Nike is often cited as an example of a firm that focuses exclusively on brand management. Nike does not own any manufacturing facilities and networks its business partners to work on production and logistics functions. This allows Nike to have a single-minded focus on its marketing activities. Most importantly, Nike can react quickly to changing customer tastes, as it does not have to retool any manufacturing facilities. Given that product life cycles are getting shorter, it becomes important to plan for competitive agility within the firm and in the supply chain. When making decisions on the acquisition of technology, a manager has to have an eye on the future with regard to potential outsourcing of noncore functions.

Evolution Not Revolution

Despite the evolutionary changes in the business environment, all three of the aforementioned enterprise models—vertical, market, and network—will continue to coexist. Many family-owned firms might never progress to hiring professional management. That does not preclude them from participating with firms in the second or third stage as a supplier or in a business network. Similarly, the mass-production model of the second evolutionary stage may be perfectly appropriate for a low-cost, high-efficiency manufacturer with predictable demand.

Conversely a firm may simultaneously use elements of the market economy model for production and elements of the network economy model for customer interaction. A firm such as Solectron, which specializes in custom electronic manufacturing, may be organized for low-cost mass production, but its customer interaction will have elements of the network model. In fact, rarely will firms will be using only one model or the other. Rather the use of each model will vary by product line and division, and will be determined by the strategic business drivers, the firm's administrative and technological heritage, and executive priorities and preferences. Contrary to the claims found in the popular business press, evolutionary progress does not mean that a form characteristic of a preceding model is replaced or irrelevant.

Traditional Supply Chain Systems

As a result of the transition to the network economy, new supply chain management terms and concepts are being introduced at a rapid pace. However, market economy supply chain systems remain relevant to firms specializing in high-volume manufacturing. Given the fact that network and market models coexist in most firms, a background in commonly used terms and corresponding technology solutions from the market economy model will help the reader understand the business and IT challenges in integrating elements of these two models.

Supply Chain Defined

A *supply chain* is a group of firms that work in a coordinated manner in procuring raw materials and components, manufacturing a product from these materials, and delivering a finished product to a customer. A typical supply chain would include raw materials suppliers, logistics firms, component manufacturers, distributors, and outsourced service firms.

Coordination across the supply chain is crucial for profitable utilization of property, plant, and equipment (PPE) and personnel across the group of firms. This implies that information about goods and services as they flow across the supply chain has to be shared and be readily available at the point of need. Further, interfirm processes have to be well defined to avoid the idling of facilities or personnel due to miscommunication. Traditional supply chains have a linear flow from the acquisition of raw materials to delivery of the finished product to consumers, as shown in Figure 1.2.

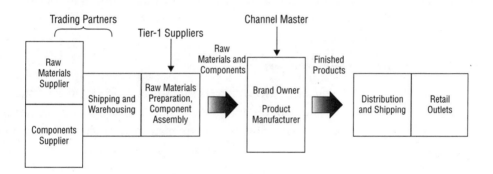

Figure 1.2: Trading partners across the supply chain.

Trading Partners and Channel Masters

The firms participating in the supply chain are referred to as channel masters or trading partners, depending on the role that they are playing. A *channel master* defines the processes for coordinated activity across the supply chain. In the previous example of a network economy firm, Nike would be the channel master. Similarly, in a manufacturing automotive environment, car companies such as Ford and General Motors are channel masters for their respective automotive supply chains. Nike sells sizable portions of its athletic footwear and apparel through retail stores operated by the

Venator Group. On the supplier side, Nike has virtually all of its products manufactured by independent contractors from multiple countries. These firms are Nike's *trading partners*. Firms such as Delphi Systems, Visteon, and Goodyear are trading partners for automotive manufacturers.

Trading partners directly interact with one another in the supply chain. For example in Figure 1.2, the raw materials supplier and shipping and warehousing are trading partners, as are the Tier-1 suppliers and the product manufacturer. The channel master is a trading partner as well, but with the power to establish processes that all the trading partners must adhere to. A Tier-1 supplier is a trading partner of the channel master. For a given product the group of firms that are part of the collaborative process depicted in the figure form the supply chain for that product. Depending on the authority exercised by the channel master, this group could be called a supply chain community, where the trading partners are working together as peers to reduce waste across the supply chain and share savings equitably. However, the arm's-length nature of transactions in the market economy model and distrust of suppliers frequently undermine the supply chain community concept.

Supply Chain Management

Supply chain management (SCM) covers the process and technology of coordinating the smooth flow of products and services among the trading partners and across the supply chain. Supply chain management is aimed at maximum utilization of every trading partner's resources (PPE, direct labor, working capital, etc). SCM is traditionally comprised of three areas. They are:

- Supply chain planning (SCP)
- Supply chain execution (SCE) systems
- Supply chain transaction (SCT) systems

Supply chain planning takes the demand forecast for a product and breaks it down into how the product is going to be manufactured and sourced. It can be thought of as a decision support tool that allows what-if planning based on the constraints within the firm and across the supply chain. Trading partners participate in planning and setting up the sourcing, manufacturing, and distribution structures to produce the forecasted demand. Supply chain planning also involves the scheduling of resources within a firm to manufacture or assemble the finished or intermediary products in a cost-effective and efficient manner. Traditional SCP functions include demand planning, planning for direct raw materials procurement and distribution, and scheduling transportation and manufacturing for optimal efficiency. Supply chain system vendors and ERP vendors have a broad range of applications targeted to these functions. Most manufacturing firms that have significant investments in PPE practice SCP for efficient utilization of their investments. Manufacturers of silicon chips for the computer and automotive industries and makers of aerospace and heavy equipment all use SCP disciplines.

Supply chain execution systems focus on reducing unplanned shipping costs and inventory holding costs. For example, JIT systems reduce working capital and inventory holding costs by procuring raw materials and components just before they are needed for production. Systems to support other supply chain execution processes address areas such as warehouse management applications and transportation management systems. The scope of these systems is such that they are able to provide services for interaction between regional and global trading partners.

Supply chain transaction systems record and integrate all information flows between the trading partners through SCM, SCE systems, or transaction systems. Transaction systems have their roots in the second evolution, the era of production efficiency. Typically a mixture of mainframe and ERP systems, they use the most mature application software, provided by a multitude of ERP vendors such as SAP, Oracle, and PeopleSoft and a host of smaller vendors offering less sophisticated point solutions.

Examining the traditional market economy model of supply chains reveals that there is tight integration across the supply chain for processes and supporting technology solutions. Such integration is necessary to manage the complex and coordinated flow of goods, services, and information across multiple trading partners. Technology solutions providing this functionality are fairly rigid and have best practices embedded in them.

Supply Chain Systems and the Product Life Cycle

Despite application vendor claims to the contrary, it is difficult to have a lean, efficient, and cost-effective market economy supply chain that is competitively flexible and allows rapid change and innovation. A discussion of the SCM functionality that is used during the life cycle of a product or service will help put these claims in perspective. (See Figure 1.3.)

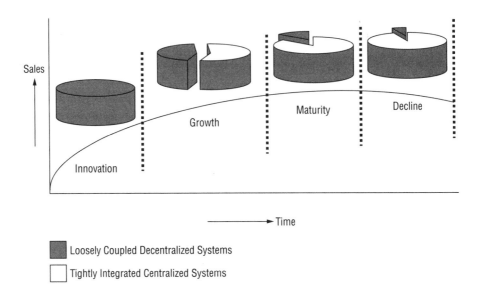

Figure 1.3: The evolution of a typical supply chain system during the life cycle of a product or service.

The product life-cycle concept is a theory that associates product sales volumes over time with different competitive conditions and possible strategic choices. The competitive conditions are usually categorized into four stages: introduction (innovation), growth, maturity, and decline. Consider the example of the VCR. Sony, Phillips, and Matsushita first introduced VCRs in the late 1960s and early 1970s. In this early (introductory) stage there were three major competitors, each with a somewhat different technology. Sales growth was slow at first because customers were uncertain about which technology to bet on. This was very important, because VCRs require the purchase of complementary goods, the videotapes. The tapes of the three competitor technologies were not compatible. Furthermore, customers were uncertain about the usefulness of this new technology. Initially, the VCR vendors envisioned that customers would use VCRs primarily to view taped films they had purchased. Although this is still a common use of the equipment, most owners of VCRs use them to view rented films and TV programs they have taped themselves. The point is that VCR sales did not begin to accelerate until the usefulness had been made clear to potential customers, the standards war was over, and equipment prices began to fall. Thus the introductory phase of a product's life cycle is characterized by high technological uncertainty and high costs associated with product development and market penetration.

Once customers are convinced of the value of the product and the product is priced correctly, sales volumes start to increase sharply. During the growth phase of the VCR, a large number of additional manufacturers, mostly from Japan and later from Korea, entered the market. A high level of additional sales was sustained until all households with a TV had at least one VCR. The rapid growth of ancillary services, such as video rental, further increased the demand for VCRs.

The product life cycle of the VCR moved into the maturity stage in the early 1980s, when most of the market was saturated. As the market matured, competitor producers started to lower prices to attract additional customers not previously targeted. Also, consumers were enticed to buy additional VCRs to be matched with other TVs in the household. Product differentiation became important, such as integrated TV/VCR sets, additional programming features, and better picture clarity. On the production side, cost efficiency became even more important and production was further outsourced to overseas manufacturers. Some of the weaker competitors exited the market. The VCR stayed in the maturity stage for almost 20 years.

The stage of decline for the VCR started in the late 1990s. The decline stage is characterized by a continued decline in sales, a further drop in prices, and even more producers exiting the market. For the VCR the decline started with the introduction of the DVD player, which provides even better picture quality, has a larger storage capacity, and offers direct rather than sequential access to programming (no tape winding required). During the last few years, DVD players have sold well, and viewable content has become available through DVD rentals. Additional challenges to the VCR are cable or satellite on-demand programming (pay-per-view). Once recordable DVDs and DVD recorders become widely available, the fate of the VCR will be sealed.

The VCR example illustrates how different strategic demands are placed on firms as their products move through the different stages in the life cycle. These different strategic demands in turn translate into different operational requirements. During the product introduction (innovation) stage, a firm uses a number of informal processes with its trading partners. Information technology solutions tend to be collaborative and allow frequent changes, as the product is refined during and after preliminary market tests. The focus is on rapid adaptability of the supply chain to consumer feedback. As the product's features and functionality stabilize after successful introduction, the focus shifts to sales growth.

In the growth phase, a firm organizes its supply chain to capture market share. The supply chain's focus shifts to support rapid growth across new customer segments and across multiple geographic locations. Formal processes and systems begin to accelerate the flow of finished product to the market. In general, at this stage of the product life cycle most enterprises acquire supply chain transaction systems. Informal, collaborative processes and technology begin to be replaced by more rigid, best-practice processes.

Market maturity places emphasis on cost efficiency and maximum utilization of PPE and working capital. Additional growth in market share comes through intense competition and at the expense of gross margins. In such a situation, a firm's profitability is improved by decreasing costs through reengineering across the supply chain. Typically the focus is on accurately forecasting and meeting market demand with minimal inventory holding costs. To achieve these goals, a great deal of integration through processes and technology has to occur across the supply chain. It is during the maturity phase that a firm begins to acquire SCP and SCE systems. Ultimately, a continued decline in sales further increases pressure to reduce costs and improve profitability. At this point, product managers feel like they are being asked to wring water from a rock. However, the bottom line may yet be improved through even finer reengineering of already reengineered processes.

Ideally during growth, but realistically during market maturity, a firm needs to make a decision whether to retire the product or jump out of the product life cycle with innovations. Unfortunately, managers will find that the supply chain systems developed during a product's march to maturity have become rigid and inflexible. This reality is faced by most enterprises that have legacy systems and products. These are the critical questions:

- How does a manager in this situation transition to the network economy model?

- Where in the life-cycle stage should you make a technology decision that allows competitive flexibility and product or service innovation?

As most managers are aware, implementing process change through technologies such as ERP is difficult enough. Consider, however, the implications of changing processes across multiple trading partners as a result of instituting a new supply chain system. These issues will be addressed in subsequent chapters.

Introduction to the Network Structure

Tightly integrated vertical firms and their supply chains are excellent at turning out high-volume, low-cost products but very poor at innovations and competitive agility. To achieve economies of scale and cost efficiency, firms need to commit to specialized PPE and supply chain technologies. In contrast, a supply chain community is a network of trading partners that come together aided by technology to develop and sustain a product or service. The trading partners in a supply chain community specialize in a core competency (be it shipping, manufacturing, marketing, billing, order entry, or procurement services). They come together as needed and disband when the product or service is no longer profitable. Note that trading partners in a network economy supply chain are loosely integrated and the relationships are closer than typical arm's-length supplier relationships.

Do such firms really exist? In the future, will all firms collaborate in network structures? Emerging network structures have been discussed in managerial and academic circles since the 1980s. Even the far-flung operations of seventeenth-century English and Dutch trading firms can be considered early forms of networks. However, while managers of the early trading firms had to rely on a physical network to coordinate activities—their numerous brothers and cousins—the pervasiveness of IT has enabled a whole new kind of network structure. Depending on products and services offered and the competitive environment, the degree to which today's firms will be involved in network relationships varies. In the aggregate, however, network structures will become ever more important tools to achieve efficiency while remaining competitively flexible. Subsequent chapters provide more detail on the appropriate network structure for a firm depending on the following issues:

- Where is the firm in the product or service life cycle?

- Who are current and future competitors?

- What is the current technology infrastructure of the firm?

Network relationships exist between firms and their suppliers and customers. However, the need for competitive flexibility also often requires that firms redefine internal relationships. Networks within firms are most prevalent today in knowledge-intensive industries, such as law firms and consulting firms and some high-tech companies. The goal of intrafirm networks is to facilitate more rapid response to changing customer demand while maintaining operational efficiency. One example of an internal network structure is a cross-functional product team that maintains functional efficiency while focusing on product and service features and customer requirements. Most importantly, lateral communications, not just top-down decision making, is promoted. Thus, the emergence of the network economy model requires firms to reexamine their relationships with their trading partners, the organizational relationships within the firm, and the boundaries of the firm.

From Supply Chains to Virtual Firms

In the evolution from the market economy model to the network economy model, a dramatic change in our understanding of supplier relationships will be required. Figure 1.4 illustrates the differences between the market economy and network economy models with regard to internal structure and degree of supply chain integration. Tightly integrated systems are appropriate for the purely efficiency-focused firms of the market economy. At the other end of the spectrum is the completely virtual firm, which relies on a network of trading partners to focus exclusively on customer needs. Very few firms will ever find themselves at either of these extremes. A typical firm may find itself with a combination of various elements of the market and network economy models dictated by the firm's competitive environment and strategic direction. The natural evolution of a network economy firm may be to a virtual enterprise that focuses on one or more core competencies and divests itself of noncore activities beyond those associated with sourcing, making, and distributing products. These activities could range from information systems maintenance to payroll processing. A "pure" virtual firm may have no physical assets at all, and instead rely on a wide network of allies who provide materials and services on a project-by-project basis. The move from vertical to virtual integration for a firm will be dictated largely by the business requirements and organizational structure of the firm. We will show that depending on the situation, either vertical or virtual integration can be a valid model for achieving competitive agility.

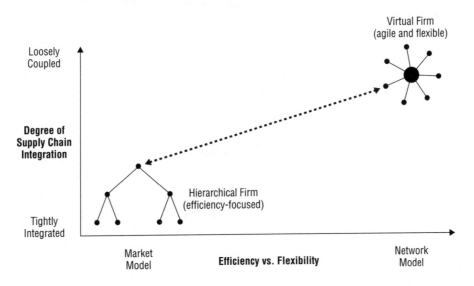

Figure 1.4: Market economy model and network economy model: Efficiency versus agility and degree of supply chain integration.

We will revisit strategic and technological issues associated with the evolution from the market to the network economy model after presenting an overview of the nature of goods and services procured by a firm in the value creation process. This discussion will set the stage for understanding the visible and invisible cost drivers across the supply chain. Finally, we will provide the practicing manager with a technology-selection framework based on trade-offs between acquisition costs, operating efficiency, competitive flexibility and agility, and responsiveness to product, service, and process innovation.

The Productive Process within the Firm

An understanding of the goods and services procured, and the value-add activities within a firm, is necessary before a manager can participate in technology and process decisions impacting the supply chain. Lack of this knowledge leads to bad decisions or worse, indecision regarding selecting supply chain solutions or participating in a trade exchange or marketplace. The trade exchange is typically sponsored by dominant channel masters within a particular industry, whereas the marketplace focuses around a particular product or service aimed at multiple industries with no dominant customers or suppliers. This chapter is a review of direct and indirect inputs into the production process within a firm. We will provide enough depth to enable the IT and general managers in their efforts to translate high-level strategy into tactical action plans. To paraphrase a common saying among executives, "My firm is no longer competing against firm A, but against firm A and its supply chain." The type of good or service procured, and its relationship to the strategic goals of the firm, drives the technology solution to meet current objectives and sets the stage for future competitive agility.

But first we need to understand the transformation process within a firm. This process is also known as the *value-add* process, and the supporting supply chain and firm are called the *value chain*. Another term for the supply chain of a firm providing services is *service chain*. The transformation process presented in Figure 2.1 applies to a firm producing products and

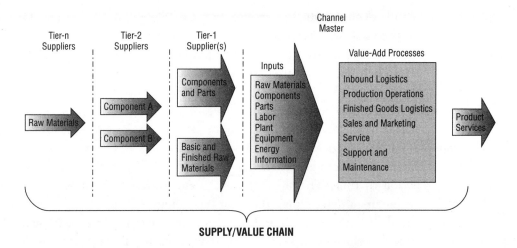

Figure 2.1: A typical supply–value-add chain for a firm producing goods and services.

services. The outputs could be products only, services only, or a combination of both. The value-add processes represent a sample of the different activities that occur within the firm. These processes will be unique to every firm and dependent on the product or service being produced.

What to call the firms shown in Figure 2.1—a supply chain, supply Web, or a service chain—will depend on the relationships between the trading partners and their degree of integration. We will make these distinctions clearer in subsequent chapters. For the remainder of this chapter, we will refer to the collection of firms shown in Figure 2.1 as a supply chain.

A typical firm buys a wide variety of goods and services—labeled "inputs" in the figure—and transforms them into products and services to sell to consumers and/or other businesses. These inputs can be basic raw materials, components, production facilities, assembly-line labor, energy, engineering services, and information. A productive system takes a variety of inputs and turns them into products or services.

For example, an airline takes as inputs airplanes, flight crews, freight, and a variety of services (e.g., passenger handling services) and uses them in the production of transportation services. Similarly, an automotive productive system takes as inputs raw materials (such as steel), prefabricated components, energy, and direct labor and uses them in the production of automobiles. The primary difference between these two productive systems is the shelf life of the product or service. In the case of an airline, an unsold air ticket becomes worthless after the aircraft departs its loading bay. Products or services aimed at a particular fashion or trend—such as platform shoes or bell-bottom trousers—tend to have short shelf lives. They are in demand only so long as the trend lasts for that particular fashion. Services in general do not have any shelf life at all. They can't be produced ahead of time and stored for consumption at a later date. Consider, for example, medical services that are needed at the time a person is sick. In contrast, an unsold automobile retains value on a dealer's parking lot for a longer period of time. The shelf life of the end product or service is an important factor in determining the right technology solution for a supply chain. The shelf lives of goods and services that a firm procures as inputs plays a role in determining such things as wastage or spoilage, inventory holding costs, etc. Let us take a closer look at some general categories of the types of goods and services that a firm procures.

Categories of Goods and Services

Mapping goods and services procured by a firm by activities directly attributable to a product or service serves to highlight the differences in the level of process and technology integration with suppliers. Figure 2.2 shows all inputs that a firm consumes in its daily activities. These inputs can be categorized into those that are directly attributable to an end product or service and those that provide general administrative and support services.

It is generally accepted that the goods and services procured by a firm can be broken down into two broad categories:

- Inputs directly attributable to the product and service
- Inputs used for administrative and support activities

In the category of inputs directly attributable to the product and service, we distinguish direct raw materials, indirect raw materials (those sourced by our suppliers), direct services, and PPE. Examples of administrative and supporting inputs are maintenance and repair, health care for workers, office supplies, and travel.

This general categorization can be applied to a firm's product or service. Further, this depiction holds true irrespective of whether the productive

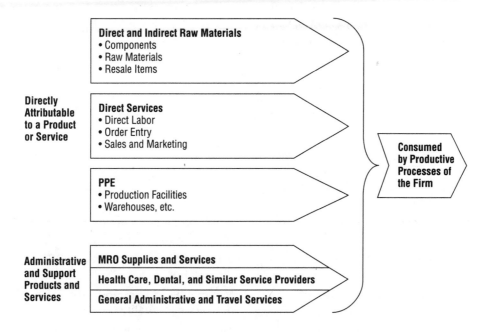

Figure 2.2: Categories of goods and services procured by a firm.

processes occur within the firm or are outsourced. The impact of sourcing the value-add activities—be they manufacturing, service delivery, or administrative services—will have an impact on the degree of process and technology integration with the outsourcing firm. Let us examine the characteristics of goods and services in these categories, starting with those directly attributable to a product or service.

Direct Raw Materials

Direct raw materials fall into two broad categories:

- Finished or component raw materials
- Basic raw materials

Consider a simplified supply chain of an automotive manufacturer. Basic raw materials are items such as iron ore or coal that a steel mill may buy to produce steel. Finished components may be door stampings, car seats, engines, etc., which an automotive manufacturer may assemble to produce a car. Finished or component raw materials have to be manufactured or finished to engineering specifications set by the automotive manufacturer. Basic raw material inputs (such as steel) that a component manufacturer buys to build components for the automotive manufacturer are considered indirect raw materials for the automotive manufacturer.

Table 2.1 shows five critical dimensions of direct raw materials that must be considered when making technology choices for the supply chain.

Table 2.1 Attributes of Direct Raw Materials

Dimensions	Impact
Dollar volume of purchases	High
Number of purchase orders	Small. Negotiated, multiyear contracts with suppliers
Impact of shortages	Critical. Idling investments in PPE, direct labor
Commoditized content	Minimal. Even commoditized content has delivery and quality targets
Integration with suppliers	Tight process and technology integration

The dollar value of purchases for direct raw materials will constitute the biggest slice of the procurement pie. Therefore percentage savings in this category tend to have great impact on business results. The number of purchase orders is an indicator of the frequency of purchases and has implications for the scalability of the supply chain system. Shortages impact system reliability, but also affect a firm's ability to efficiently tap alternative sources for the input. Commoditized content also affects the extent to which a firm is able to switch to alternate suppliers. Finally, integration with suppliers is an indicator of the extent to which a firm needs to coordinate its systems with those of the suppliers and the mutual dependency in the supply chain system.

It is estimated that firms spend anywhere from 40 to 75 percent of their revenue on purchasing raw materials, components, and services from other firms. Direct raw materials also constitute the biggest item in terms of dollar volume for a typical firm in the manufacturing sector. Another characteristic for the purchase of direct raw materials is the relatively low number of purchase orders. Given the importance of these materials to the production process of the firm, it becomes essential to have negotiated purchase orders for the firm's planning horizon to meet projected production schedules. For component manufacturers it becomes necessary to meet required delivery schedules and engineering specifications.

If the raw materials are not delivered to meet the production schedule of the firm, there can be substantial losses in terms of underutilization of PPE. Other losses that may occur are wages paid to direct labor and opportunity costs at the sales end due to shortages of goods or services. Raw materials that do not meet quality and engineering specifications have two possible outcomes:

- The first is to not put the raw material into the production process, thereby idling PPE. The economic impact would be the same as having no raw material in the first place, as described previously.

- The second outcome would be to run the production lines with the substandard raw materials. The impact of doing this would be realized after the sale of the product or service, resulting in excessive warranty or product recall costs due to substandard raw materials in the product.

All Nuts Are Not Created Equal

Another important characteristic is the commoditized content in raw materials. *Commodities* are goods and services whose characteristics are widely known, and substitutes from a variety of manufacturers and suppliers are available. A 60-watt light bulb is an example of a commodity item. A consumer has a choice of suppliers, but the commodity item being procured is a 60-watt light bulb. Even though many of the direct raw materials may appear to be commodities without any specialized characteristics, quality and delivery requirements make them unique and critical to a firm's operations.

The following anecdote from a farm equipment manufacturing plant illustrates this point. A production plant supervisor had a big sign at the manufacturing plant's entrance that said, "All nuts are not created equal!!" On inquiry about the meaning behind the sign, it transpired that the supervisor was fighting a battle with the firm's purchasing department over nuts needed for the production process. The purchasing group wanted to award a contract for nuts needed in the production process to an overseas supplier who had submitted the lowest bid. Even though the nuts were a commodity item, the current supplier delivered and stocked 2000 nuts every day in various bins located in the production facility. The overseas supplier did not offer those services and in addition could not guarantee delivery to synchronize with the weekly production schedule. Compounding the problem was a lack of space at the plant to stock more than 4 days' supply of nuts. Lastly, shortages due to missed deliveries or substandard quality would mean idling the entire production line with negative economic consequences for the plant. The supervisor was quite right. "All nuts are not created equal!! Production nuts are strategic."

The final characteristic of raw materials is degree of integration with suppliers. Depending on the extent to which an input is critical to a firm's output, and the degree to which a supplier is involved in component design and engineering, there may be tight integration of processes and technology—at least with Tier-1 suppliers. Changes in product design to meet market requirements necessitate rapid and coordinated communication with the suppliers. Close communication and coordination are also required to manage the tricky balancing act of keeping enough inventory in the pipeline to meet production schedules, but not too much to incur excessive inventory holding costs.

Asset utilization, inventory holding, and shipping and transportation costs have been some of the business problems addressed by materials requirements planning (MRP), manufacturing resource planning (MRP II), ERP, and supply chain systems. From an information technology solutions standpoint, this area has received much attention over the past few decades. The foundation for most of the supply chain solutions are established and proven best practices, coordinating the flow of raw materials across multiple firms.

Direct Services

In the service sector, but also for manufacturing firms, direct services are a significant part of the total spending of a firm. For ease of exposition, we will use the term *direct services* to encompass all service activities that can be mapped directly to the manufacture and sales of a specific product or service that a firm produces. However, we must distinguish between two types of direct services, services that are required for a typical manufacturing firm and those used by a services firm. Table 2.2 shows the five dimensions that were previously listed for direct raw materials and their characteristics for both a manufacturing firm and a services firm.

Table 2.2 Attributes of Direct Services

Dimension	Impact on Manufacturing Firm	Impact on Services Firm
Dollar volume of purchases	Low to medium	High
Number of purchase orders	Low to medium	High
Impact of shortages	Moderate. Mitigate with extra shifts and redeployment of personnel	Critical. Typically leads to unfilled orders or underutilization of fixed assets
Commoditized content	Low. Requires training and certification to handle production equipment	Medium. Certified, trained professionals can be substituted
Integration with suppliers	Moderate	Moderate

Direct services in a manufacturing environment are comprised mainly of direct labor needed to work in the production facilities. For most large manufacturing firms, the dollar volume of direct labor purchases is lower than that of direct materials. There has been a growing trend to outsource the direct labor services to contingent staffing firms, such as Manpower and Kelly Services. This holds especially true for light industrial manufacturers. These types of outsourcing arrangements tend to be long term in nature and cover an entire region or country to make vendor management easier.

The impact of direct labor shortages in this environment is moderate. When facing labor shortages, measures such as additional shifts or redeployment of administrative staff can typically address the problem in the short term. The commoditized content of this labor pool is relatively low, as people can't easily be shifted from one manufacturing task to another without some basic level of retraining. In less-skilled, light industrial jobs, it is feasible to cross-train and redeploy personnel for other duties at a nominal expense. Specialized labor that needs a high degree of skill or certification is typically procured by a long-term contract or full-time employment with the manufacturing firm to ensure that the production lines run without interruptions.

Direct labor costs in a typical service firm tend to be very high. These costs may range from 40 to 70 percent of revenue. Consider the contingency staffing industry, which has gross margins of 4 to 9 percent. The volume of direct labor purchases is very high and so is the recruiting expense. The number of purchase orders in this instance translates to the number of recruitment efforts needed to fill open positions. This is one of the biggest expense items for a service firm, and employee retention is key to profitability.

A shortage of direct labor will have an immediate impact on revenues and profitability for service firms. Consider the example of airline services. Without a trained and qualified air crew or maintenance personnel, aircraft will be grounded. In addition to the lost revenue and goodwill due to cancelled flights, the fixed costs of the airplane also have to be considered. Thus both costs and revenues are negatively affected.

Many service jobs also require a higher degree of training, particularly in knowledge industries such as consulting or IT services. Service chain solutions (analogous to supply chains in the manufacturing sector) to recruit and retain direct labor are slowly beginning to address this area. Suppliers in the service chain tend to be training providers, recruiting agencies, specialized benefit providers, etc. Increasingly there is a move to collaborate with suppliers across the service chain to reduce costs. The integration within the service chain differs significantly compared to the supply chain in the manufacturing context. In the service chain, a firm is providing services within the context of business processes of customers—which calls for collaboration rather than integration.

Property, Plant, and Equipment

Because of the importance and cost impact of past investments in PPE, traditional supply chain technology solutions have primarily focused on developing systems to enhance the flow of direct raw materials. There are few applications geared to the procurement of PPE itself, which encompasses all the fixed assets needed to produce and deliver a firm's products and services. Investments in appropriate PPE allow a firm to be efficient in achieving its strategic goals. Such efficiency is required to remain competitive in the market. On the flip side, cumulative investments in specialized PPE can inhibit the development and deployment of new product innovations, because the cost to modify existing PPE may be too high. Especially in light of increasingly shorter product life cycles, shorter product development, and global competition, it is important to understand this trade-off between low production costs and competitive agility. The *competitive agility* of a firm is its ability to react rapidly to changes in its external environment as a result of actions by the firm's competitors, suppliers, and customers, as well as the commercial viability of substitute products that become competitors to the firm's product line. When faced with such external changes, the firm's ability to take action to defend its market share or differentiate its product line or find alternative raw material sourcing is dependent largely on its ability to react quickly. The ability to rapidly change organizational structure, processes, and productive technologies to meet external challenges is a measure of the firm's competitive agility. Tightly integrated processes and PPE aimed at being the lowest-cost producer will, in general, inhibit the competitive agility of a firm.

This trade-off has to be kept in mind when selecting the technology infrastructure necessary to allow a firm flexibility while the market for its product or service becomes mature or even declines. Table 2.3 shows the characteristics of PPE along the five dimensions.

Table 2.3 Characteristics of Property, Plant, and Equipment

Dimension	Impact
Dollar volume of purchases	Very high
Number of purchase orders	Low
Impact of shortages	Moderate to high. PPE purchases are usually complex and require the coordination of many vendors
Commoditized content	Low. PPE is usually very customized
Integration with suppliers	Moderate to high. Requires customization, coordination with other vendors, and tight scheduling

Examples of PPE are assets involved in turning direct labor and raw materials into products and services. Representative of this category are capital items, such as factories, assembly lines, and specialized manufacturing equipment; transportation; assets; and information systems supporting procurement, production, and service delivery. The dollar volume of these types of purchases is very high, but tends to occur at irregular intervals in a firm's life. In contrast, purchase of direct labor and raw materials occurs at regular intervals to meet production schedules. Acquiring, installing, and commissioning PPE tends to be a one-time affair, often requiring a high degree of collaboration and interaction with suppliers. Putting PPE in service requires tight scheduling to coordinate the work of multiple suppliers in getting the production facilities commissioned on time. The work is very knowledge-intensive and project-focused.

Consider a computer chip factory. They periodically introduce new chips that require substantial investments in PPE. The production facilities can't have dust or other impurities. The chip fabrication equipment costs are significant. The goal of the chip manufacturer when building a factory is to ensure that the PPE is put to use as quickly as possible. Obviously, much will depend on the sequencing of construction and equipment roll-out. These factors can be quite complex for a chip factory and require sophisticated project management. To put this in perspective, let us look at building a house. Before the house can be built, the plans have to be approved by the local authority. Contractors for all aspects of the job—the foundation work, carpentry, plumbers, electricians, drywall hangers, bricklayers, masonry work, painting, etc.—have to be located and their work scheduled. Carpentry can't occur before the foundation is laid. Plumbers and electricians have to perform their work before the drywall is hung. There is a sequence of events that dictate the building of a house. It is in the home builder's interest to get the construction over with as quickly as possible so the family can move in. In reality, the construction of the house may languish and move at snail's pace for months on end. This typically occurs because a particular craftsperson on the critical path is not available according to the schedule. The plumbing contractor may not be available for a period of weeks. Drywall and flooring have to wait until the plumbing is finished. By the time the plumbing is completed, the drywall contractor may have scheduling conflicts. Every time that a contractor on the critical path causes delay, there is a snowball effect on other dependent activities. Meanwhile, the home builder may have moved out of a rental property and be staying in a hotel at considerable expense. For a computer chip factory, these types of delays can mean millions of dollars tied up in unproductive, work-in-process physical plant. Delays in building and commissioning PPE rapidly have significant economic penalties for a firm.

Maintenance, Repair, and Operating Supplies

The last significant area of goods and services procured by a firm is comprised of MRO and support and administrative services. The most distinguishing feature of this category is that it has the lowest dollar volume per purchase but has the highest number of transactions. Unbeknownst to most companies, the cost of processing a typical transaction in this category is greater than the cost of the item being acquired. Thus, there exists great scope for process reengineering, automation, or outsourcing.

In most firms, MRO purchasing generates the maximum number of purchase orders. The associated administrative work in terms of qualifying vendors, approving purchases, and ordering, receiving, auditing, and paying for these purchases is substantial. Conversely, this huge number of transactions has the smallest share of the annual costs in a firm. Table 2.4 illustrates the major categories within the MRO area along our five dimensions. Note that the dollar volume has been combined with the risk dimension for ease of exposition.

Table 2.4 Attributes of Different MRO Categories

Dimension	Low Dollar Volume, Low Risk	Low Dollar Volume, High Risk	High Dollar Volume, Low Risk	High Dollar Volume, High Risk
Products and services	Training materials, promotional items, PR services	Lubricants, plant consumables	Office productivity software, facilities	Communications, engineering equipment, ERP
Number of purchase orders	High	Low	Moderate	Low
Impact of shortages	Low	Critical	Low	Significant
Commoditized content	High	Medium	High	Medium
Integration with suppliers	Low	Moderate	Low	High

Examples of low-dollar-volume, low-risk MRO items are training materials, promotional items, and accessories. This category generates a significant number of purchase orders and associated administrative work. There is little predictability to these purchases and they are procured as needed within a firm. In case of shortage or unavailability of these MRO items, there is very little impact to ongoing operations or productive processes of the firm. The amount of customization for this category is minimal. For example, it may involve putting a firm's logo on coffee mugs. For the most part, the items in this category are commodities with multiple substitutes and suppliers. Integration with suppliers is low due to the nonstrategic nature and high availability of these items from multiple sources. For this category, the following statement rings true, "Requisitioning, ordering, receiving, and paying through traditional means may cost more than the item itself."

Low-dollar-volume, high-risk MRO items, while not very expensive, have the effect of disrupting operations if there is a shortfall. Operating consumables, such as lubricants needed to keep production machinery in good repair, are examples from this category. Lack of ready availability of these items at the point and time of need can seriously cripple ongoing operations. The number of purchase orders is significantly lower than for the preceding category of MRO items. Given the importance of the materials to the production process, agreements with suppliers tend to have delivery and quality expectations. Even though most items in this category are commodities, from an operational perspective, because of delivery and quality requirements, they are de-commoditized. There is a moderate level of integration with suppliers for contingency support in case of shortages. This category is analogous to the "All nuts are not equal!!" category of direct raw materials.

Office productivity software, PCs, and professional services fall into the category of high-dollar-volume, low-risk purchases. They are typically of high value, but have minimal impact on the productive operations within a firm. The number of transactions for this category tends to be significant, as most demand for this category occurs at the local branch or department level. Purchase decisions tend to be decentralized, usually based on standards set by corporate headquarters. These items tend to be commodities with multiple substitutes. A major driver for trying to standardize on a particular product brand is to reduce the long-term cost of maintenance and support—especially in the office automation area. Integration with suppliers is minimal, given the arm's-length nature of the transactions involved.

Finally, the last category—high-dollar-volume, high-risk purchases—is the most significant from the perspective of its impact on a firm's long-term strategic goals. Representative items include complex ERP systems, engineering systems (e.g., CAD/CAM), and communications systems (e.g., wide-area networks [WANs]). Shortages do not have an immediate impact on the productive operations of the firm. However, improper implementation or implementation failures from systems such as ERP can have an adverse impact on a firm's ability to achieve its strategic goals. The number of purchase orders and transactions tends to be low for this category. The duration of the contract may be spread over a period of years until the complex system is fully implemented and operational. Integration with suppliers during this period tends to support training, troubleshooting, and knowledge transfer efforts. The biggest risk stems from inappropriate system choices and implementation failures. Inappropriate system choices to support a complex application can result in implementation failures or delays until the mistake is rectified. The popular press reported incidents of many firms that allowed access to their internal systems (such as order placement and account status) to customers through the Internet that failed publicly. Initially, some of these firms didn't correctly assess the impact of customer queries on their corporate firewall and internal WAN. Their internal WAN was used to link key operational systems, and the sudden influx of customer-generated traffic brought many firewalls and internal WANs to their knees. Typically, operational systems within such firms were adversely impacted by the customer traffic. The customers were dissatisfied with the response time from the corporate Web site, the internal functions within the firm suffered, and the firm suffered financial losses. An appropriate firewall to support the customer traffic and routing could have avoided these failures.

Administrative and Support Services

Administrative and professional services span the spectrum not covered by the preceding categories. They range from human resources recruitment services, dental and health care services, and corporate travel and lodging. We distinguish two types of services: those that are highly customized to a firm's requirements and those that are commoditized. Health care, for example, is usually customized. Typically health care service contracts last over a period of years, with very detailed contractual terms and conditions regarding the nature of services provided. Travel and related services (e.g., hotels and car rental), on the other hand, have become commoditized to the extent that many firms use online services to reduce their internal administrative overhead.

Many of the service providers have varying degrees of integration into the buying firm's processes and systems. In our travel services example, the travel agency may be integrated into the email, approval, and accounting system within the firm. Similarly, the health care services provider's self-administrative functions (such as claim submissions) may be available from within the standard corporate desktop environment. Internet technologies used to connect disparate information systems within a firm are called intranets. Extranets use similar technologies and connect systems across multiple firms. Extranets and intranets are secured in that they are not part of the open Internet accessible by anyone with a browser. Extranets and intranets are secured with a variety of log-on, authentication, and firewall features. Extranets and intranets used to link functions within and across firms have demonstrated quick and measurable return on investment. However, scaling these technologies to handle significant amounts of transactions has been a problem. We will review technologies that allow this integration rapidly in Chapter 7.

Now that we have a broad overview of the characteristics of different goods and services that a firm procures, we can better understand the visible and invisible costs of procuring each major category. The dollar volume of purchases has a great impact on the extent to which price advantages will affect the firm's bottom line. The number of purchase orders indicates whether automation or outsourcing is a strategic option. Criticality of the product or service to ongoing operations has to be factored into any decision making regarding reengineering or automation. Further, it will become evident that certain spot purchases of raw materials, yielding significant price advantages, will have to be balanced with timing and delivery constraints. The higher the degree of commoditized content, the more likely we will be able to conduct spot purchases or switch suppliers. Finally, integration with suppliers is crucial to consider when designing automation options.

C H A P T E R 3

Avoidable Costs in the Supply Chain

A typical firm spends between 50 and 70 percent of its total revenues on outside purchases of goods and services. Even modest cost reductions achieved in purchasing have a profound impact on a firm's bottom line. A quote from a *CIO Magazine* article illustrates this point: "Savings in procurement have a way of thundering, rather than trickling to the bottom line."[1] The article gives a hypothetical example where a firm with $5 billion in revenue could add $20 million to its bottom line and $450 million to its market value by reducing its total procurement costs by 5 percent. Reducing total procurement costs involves effective and efficient SCM through processes and technology. But before addressing SCM processes and technology, it is important to understand the avoidable costs involved in procuring goods and services within a firm. This understanding is crucial to selecting the appropriate processes and technologies to realize the potential for huge profit improvements.

Chapter 2's exposition of the characteristics of the goods and services procured by a firm revealed that in most firms, MRO purchasing was responsible for generating the maximum amount of purchasing-related administrative work while accounting for a small part of the total dollar volume spent on purchases. For example, a firm that processes millions of invoices a year will typically find that 75 percent of them are for items less

---

[1] "The Big Payoff," *CIO Magazine*, Oct. 1, 2000, pp. 101–102.

than $1000. With traditional purchasing practices, a firm would incur a fixed cost of $100 to process the purchase order, irrespective of whether the purchase was a $2 box of paper clips or a $2000 PC. This is an example of the visible costs of procurement.

Figure 3.1 illustrates the visible and invisible costs of procuring goods and services within a firm. It is important to note that the biggest impact on the profitability of a firm is a reduction in invisible costs.

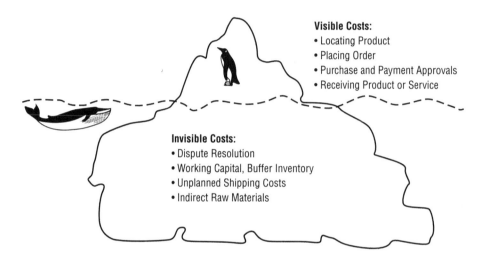

Figure 3.1: Visible and invisible costs within the firm and across the supply chain.

A major part of the total procurement expenditure of a firm is spent on direct raw materials and services. It follows that a significant part of the invisible costs of procurement occurs in this category of goods and services. The term *invisible costs* refers to avoidable costs, across the supply chains, which are not readily apparent. To reveal the invisible costs, we need to conduct a detailed study of the supply chain and procurement processes, practices, and policies. A closer examination of Figure 3.1 reveals that visible costs, such as locating a product or placing an order, are all related to the transaction processes involved in procurement. Invisible costs, such as dispute resolution, involve the nature of the supplier-buyer relationship. This difference is significant, because it dictates the types of process and technology solutions needed to address the issue of avoidable costs. Below, we will review examples from the categories of goods and services that a firm procures, identify related visible and invisible costs, and conclude with recommendations on reducing the costs associated with a particular product or service category.

Visible Costs

Traditional methods of buying low-value commodity items illustrate the visible cost factors very well. According to an article by Simon Croon in *The Journal of Supply Chain Management*, administrative costs associated with locating and requisitioning MRO–type products drop by over 60 percent when switching over to an automated Web-based system.[2] To illustrate the traditional approach and its associated avoidable costs, let us look at the case of John Requisitioner in a typical Fortune 500–type firm.

The Case of the Static Wipes

John Requisitioner and his department were recently given networked PCs. The computer monitors attracted a lot of dust and needed frequent cleaning. John also had a PC at home, which he kept dust-free by using static wipes. The static wipes not only cleaned the computer screen, but also reduced its proclivity to attract more dust particles, making frequent cleaning unnecessary. John suggested that his firm buy similar wipes for use in his department. When he volunteered to go to the local office supplies store and pick up a carton, he was told by his supervisor not to do so. John was informed that the purchasing department wanted to know about these purchases so that they could aggregate the buy and negotiate lower prices for the firm as a whole. John's supervisor instructed him to complete a requisition form for the static wipes and drop it off on his table.

Locating the Item and Placing the Order

When filling out the form, John quickly got through the section requesting information about the requisitioner's name, department, and shipping address. Then he ran into a problem with the section asking for item codes, qualified supplier name, estimated purchase price, and shipping costs. He called his corporate purchasing department for help. The purchasing department did not have the information John needed and instead asked

---

[2] Simon R. Croon, "Impact of Web Based Procurement on the Management of Operating Resources Supply," *Journal of Supply Chain Management*, Winter 2000, pp. 4–13.

him to directly contact corporate authorized suppliers. John had to wait for a couple of days for the approved suppliers list to reach him via interoffice mail from the purchasing department, which was located at the firm's headquarters 500 miles away in a different city.

He called the approved suppliers on the list to find out who could supply the static wipes. He was dismayed to learn that none of the authorized suppliers sold static wipes. John called the purchasing department to report the bad news and to inquire if he could use departmental petty cash to buy the static wipes from the local office supplies store. Current practice in John's firm was to buy office supplies in bulk every quarter and send them to branch offices and departments. The purchasing department denied John's request for acquiring the wipes with petty cash, stating that this item was going to be a repeat buy and needed by other departments as well. The purchase of static wipes should be aggregated across the entire firm to get quantity discounts. Purchasing would take on the task of inviting and qualifying vendors to supply static wipes. In the interim John was asked to give the approximate costs for the wipes and leave the supplier information blank on the requisition form.

The Approval Process

Finally, John took the partially filled requisition form to his supervisor, who signed it and passed it on to the finance department for approval and processing. John was relieved to see the last of the form, as it had taken him over 3 weeks to fill it out, in addition to numerous phone calls to suppliers and the purchasing department. He computed that he had spent over 4 hours during the past 3 weeks trying to get static wipes. He was paid at an hourly rate of $35, and a case of static wipes at his local store cost $53. His supervisor joked that if he docked John's pay for the effort needed to order the wipes, they could have picked up two cases at the local store.

After a couple more weeks of waiting for word on the static wipes, John called the purchasing department to find out when he would be receiving the shipment. The purchasing clerk had not received an approved requisition and directed John to the finance department. After multiple transfers within the finance department, John was able to track down the requisition to a financial analyst's desk. On inquiring on the approval status, John was dismayed to learn that the requisition had not been routed for approval because the form was incomplete and missing information about the supplier. John explained the situation about lack of qualified suppliers on file and the purchasing department's ongoing efforts to qualify a vendor for that purchase. The financial analyst was helpful and asked John to write a memo to that effect and send it to his attention. It took another week for the memo to thread its way through interoffice mail and become part of John's requisition for static wipes. The financial analyst told John that the approval committee met every other week, and that his requisition would be reviewed at that time.

A few more months had come and gone since John's original request to buy a case of static wipes. Frustrated by the amount of follow-up needed to buy a simple item, John got his supervisor's permission to increase the number of cases of static wipes requested because he did not wish to go through this process again. His supervisor gladly sent an email to the financial analyst to that effect. A week later John was stopped by his supervisor in the hall and informed that the static wipe requisition had been returned to him for approval from his manager. Apparently, the increase in the quantity of static wipe cases pushed the estimated dollar value of the purchase beyond the supervisor's authorization limit. Instead of seeking yet another approval, John and his supervisor reduced the number of cases, so that the dollar amount of the purchase remained within the supervisor's approval limit. The amended requisition form was sent back to the finance department for approval.

After another couple of weeks, John was gratified to hear from purchasing that the approved requisition form had been received from finance. Now the purchasing department was all set to initiate the firm's vendor qualification process, which included, among other requirements, the need to obtain three qualified bids before a purchase order could be issued. This qualification and selection process took another 2 weeks. After repeated calls, John was informed that a price competitive bid had been awarded to Acme office supplies for 15 cases of static wipes. John was overjoyed and called Acme to ask when the wipes were going to be shipped to his location.

Receiving Product and Payment Approval

Acme called John after 2 days to inform him that the wipes had been shipped and to expect them to arrive at his location the next day. There was an air of excitement in the department as everyone had been following John's quixotic quest for static wipes over the past few months with good humor. They planned a "static wipe" welcome reception in the break room and wanted to recognize John and his supervisor for perseverance and adherence to corporate purchasing procedures.

The next day, on inquiring with the mailroom, John was dismayed to find out that the wipes had not been received. He called Acme to verify the shipping status and learned that the shipment had not been accepted at the firm's receiving dock. On contacting the receiving supervisor, John was informed that in order to accept shipments, receiving had to have a matching purchase order on file at the dock. The shipment had arrived in the morning, but a matching order could not be found, so the shipment was rejected. Later that day, the receiving supervisor did receive the purchase order for the wipes in interoffice mail. The purchasing department had faxed the order to Acme and sent a copy via interoffice mail to the receiving dock.

Frustrated, John volunteered to drive by Acme after work and pick up the cases of static wipes. The receiving dock supervisor stopped him from doing so, because it would not only violate company audit policy, but also ensure that Acme would never get paid. The accounting department would never release payment to Acme unless they had a receipt acknowledgment from the receiving dock with a matching purchase order. Instead, John called up Acme and asked them to try delivering the product again. Acme wanted confirmation from John that they would be reimbursed for the additional delivery charges, as they were not included in the original purchase order. On getting assurances from John and his supervisor, Acme confirmed the shipment was scheduled for delivery later that day.

Payment to the Supplier

Finally, the cases of static wipes were delivered to John's department. John and his supervisor breathed a sigh of relief and vowed never to go through the purchasing process again. During this long odyssey, John's supervisor had discovered that other departments used petty cash and other discretionary budgets to creatively purchase goods and services, by-passing the onerous corporate purchasing process. John found himself with enough static wipes to meet his department's needs for the next couple of years. Unfortunately, the saga did not end, as Acme kept calling John to help with the payment after a few weeks had passed. The terms of the purchase order were net 30 days after receipt. Sixty days had passed since Acme's shipment, and they had yet to receive payment. When John wearily called accounts payable, he discovered that they had held up payment of Acme's invoice because the invoice amount did not match the original purchase order. Obviously, this discrepancy was due to the extra freight charges caused by the firm's refusal to accept shipment the first time around. John called finance to intervene and release payment to Acme. The entire process from the time John requisitioned the static wipes to final payment to supplier had taken over 6 months.

Lessons from the Case Example

The preceding case study is not an exaggeration, but a reflection of reality in most large organizations. The amount of time and effort expended by John, his supervisor, the financial analyst, the purchasing group, the receiving dock supervisor, and the accounts payable clerk to purchase a relatively low-dollar-value item is enormous. Clearly there is opportunity to aggregate the purchase of similar products and services across the firm to obtain price reductions and better terms. The avoidable costs that are apparent in John's firm are:

- Costs of locating and ordering products
- Approval processes—for placing order, approval of purchase, releasing payment
- Supplier qualification costs
- Receiving costs

We will present various strategies for reducing these visible costs of procuring goods and services by category of product or service. The approach and technologies to support the cost reduction strategies is influenced by the category. Before we do that, let us get a better understanding of the invisible costs in the procurement process.

Invisible Costs

Visible costs in the supply chain are primarily associated with transaction-processing activities. As we discussed in Chapter 2, MRO items are responsible for the majority of transactions in a firm, while accounting only for a small part of the total dollar volume spent on outside purchases of goods and service. Visible costs are apparent in various transaction-processing activities such as requisitioning, ordering, auditing, invoice, and payment processing. These visible costs can be decreased with efficient transaction processes supported by IT solutions. In our prior discussions, we identified purchase of direct raw materials and services as accounting for a major part of the total dollars spent by a firm. It follows from this that the biggest cost reductions are possible in this category and that the majority of these costs are invisible.

Recall that Table 2.1 showed that the number of transactions for direct raw materials and services is low and prenegotiated. Because the volume of transaction processing is low, associated cost reductions do not have a great impact on the bottom line. Instead we need to focus on the hidden costs associated with the flow of these goods and services across the supply chain. Identifying these invisible costs requires a detailed study of the purchasing and productive processes of all trading partners across the supply chain. Once these invisible costs have been discovered, reducing them requires far-reaching changes at the firm level, as it relates to interaction, trust, and information exchange between trading partners.

To illustrate cost avoidance strategies, let us look at a few representative examples of invisible costs. We will start by examining costs that are fairly evident after a preliminary examination of the supply chain and then move to those costs that need detailed study to uncover. The following examples presented do not cover the entire spectrum of invisible costs that are hidden in a particular supply chain. Supply chains for different products and services have their own unique configuration of productive processes of trading partners. This makes it difficult to identify generally applicable invisible cost areas, as they are dictated by the specific product and service being produced. Contrast this with the visible costs of procuring MRO goods and services, which are broadly applicable to most firms irrespective of the final goods being manufactured or services being offered by the firms. This is an important difference to bear in mind while we look at some representative examples of invisible costs.

Invisible Costs in Dispute Resolution

Costs associated with dispute resolution occur for most categories of products and services. For MRO–type commodity items, dispute resolution processes are covered in the standard terms and conditions. Because of the number of vendors and the volume of transactions involved, an efficient and standardized resolution process results in dramatic cost savings.

Given the huge dollar amounts spent on direct raw materials and services, having a detailed and easy-to-follow dispute resolution process has the potential for significant financial impact. Dispute resolution processes for this category are unique and are dictated by the specific product or service involved.

Disputes arise in the procurement of all goods and services that a firm buys. Most procurement processes are designed and implemented for transactions that occur as intended, but are not designed to handle exceptions. A dispute arises when a product or service does not meet the expectations of the requisitioner. These unmet expectations may vary across the spectrum from defective products, to substandard service, to delayed delivery, to incorrect billing. Analyzing the work content of most accounts payable departments, accounts receivable departments, and return merchandise authorization departments reveals that a significant amount of administrative work associated with disputes can be solved if the terms and conditions for dispute resolution are well thought out and implemented before transactions across the supply chain are initiated.

In many instances, firms prefer to write off disputed purchases because the cost of resolving them often exceeds the cost of the items in dispute. This issue is of critical importance with the increase of online marketplaces and Web-based transaction systems. These Web-based procurement systems will increase the velocity of transactions between participating firms across the supply chain or trade exchange. It is reasonable to assume that the number of transactions in dispute will also increase significantly. Disputes may be over late shipments, poor-quality products, incorrect delivery addresses, and so on.

Clearly documented and carefully implemented dispute resolution processes (automated where feasible with minimal manual intervention) will reduce the administrative costs associated with the increased velocity and volume of transactions. For non-MRO commodity items, establishing such a process requires a detailed study of the terms and conditions for every individual product and service. Obviously, electronic goods such as capacitors will have entirely different terms, conditions, and dispute resolution processes from perishable goods such as fruits and vegetables. The underlying technology to support dispute resolution processes for a firm and its supply chain partners will need to be flexible and user-configurable. Common technology solutions include work-flow-based collaborative infrastructures.

Invisible Costs and Direct Raw Materials

Working capital, buffer inventory, and unplanned shipping costs are the most common invisible costs associated with direct raw materials. A typical enterprise spends approximately 60 percent of its revenues on goods and services purchased from its Tier-1 suppliers. Similarly, a Tier-1 supplier typically spends 60 percent of its revenue (from the channel master) on purchases from Tier-2 suppliers. This translates into 36 percent (60 percent of 60 percent) of the purchase dollars of the channel master. Opportunities for savings are less visible the further we go down the supply chain.

To illustrate the invisible cost factors, let us consider Figure 3.2. A fortunate Tier-2 supplier may be connected to a Tier-1 supplier via electronic methods such as electronic data interchange (EDI) to receive electronic orders. Generally in the manufacturing sector, the orders could be received

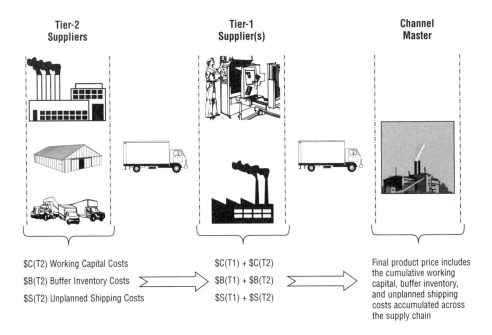

Tier-2 Suppliers	Tier-1 Supplier(s)	Channel Master
$C(T2) Working Capital Costs	$C(T1) + $C(T2)	Final product price includes the cumulative working capital, buffer inventory, and unplanned shipping costs accumulated across the supply chain
$B(T2) Buffer Inventory Costs	$B(T1) + $B(T2)	
$S(T2) Unplanned Shipping Costs	$S(T1) + $S(T2)	

Figure 3.2: Invisible cost buildup across the supply chain.

via phone, U.S. mail, or fax at the Tier-2 supplier. The Tier-2 supplier does not have direct access to the channel master's production schedule, but the Tier-1 supplier releases that information to the Tier-2 supplier on a periodic basis (weekly or monthly). Because not being able to meet the Tier-1 supplier's needs may have the negative consequence of the Tier-2 supplier being dropped from the supply chain, the Tier-2 supplier has multiple variations of components in stock to support the demand variations of the Tier-1 supplier. The unfinished components cost money to acquire and store. Working capital for these components is factored into the prices of the goods and services provided to the Tier-1 supplier.

Similarly, unplanned shipping of components due to communication trickling down slowly across the supply chain (such as next-day courier) costs more than regularly planned freight. Finally, the Tier-2 supplier also holds a buffer inventory of finished goods, just in case they are unable to meet the requirements of the Tier-1 supplier. Buffer inventory ties up additional capital, generating costs that are also factored into the price of products shipped to the Tier-1 supplier.

In Figure 3.2, these costs are depicted as $C(T2) + $B(T2) + $S(T2). The Tier-2 supplier has to pass these costs on to the Tier-1 supplier or risk going out of business. The Tier-1 supplier faces a similar dilemma, with the magnitude being lesser than for Tier-2 suppliers. Generally, the information linkages between the channel master and Tier-1 suppliers tend to be well developed. As illustrated in Figure 3.2, Tier-1 firms roll up their working capital, unplanned shipping, and buffer inventory costs into the final product price that they charge to the channel master. If one factors in the corresponding costs from Tier-3 and Tier-4 suppliers, it becomes evident that in the aggregate these constitute a big part of the submerged iceberg shown in Figure 3.1.

To reduce these costs, the technology and process solutions for trading partners (especially for Tier-2, Tier-3, etc.) need to have partner relationships in place that are rich in information sharing. Sharing specific production planning information and availability of production capacity among the trading partners is essential to identifying and reducing these costs. Without agreements in place to ensure sharing of necessary information, technology solutions will be ineffective in reducing these costs. In return for adequate planning information from the channel master, the tiered suppliers have to trade in their buffer inventory insurance and pass on those savings across the supply chain to the channel master. Thus the supplier relationship becomes redefined based on mutual trust and partnership. Without this fundamental redefinition of the trading partner relationship, *it will be difficult to identify, let alone reduce, the invisible costs*. Because a major part of the total costs incurred by a firm are in the area of direct raw materials and services, specific process and technology solutions to address associated visible and invisible cost reductions are discussed in greater detail in Chapters 4 and 5.

There are many more instances of these types of invisible costs that become apparent on close examination of the unique configuration of the supply chain for a particular product or service. Prior to the advent of cheap and ubiquitous Internet access, there was not an affordable mechanism to coordinate the flow of goods and services across the supply chain. The category of invisible costs that were reviewed in this section occurs primarily as a result of lack of information sharing. Let us now look at another category, which is a major part of the submerged iceberg in Figure 3.1: the prices paid for direct raw materials and services across all trading partners.

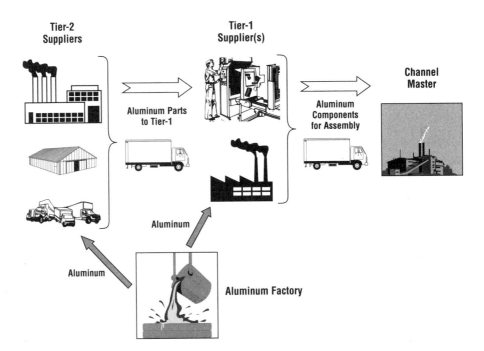

Figure 3.3: Indirect raw materials purchased across the supply chain.

Invisible Costs and Indirect Raw Materials

Indirect raw materials are raw materials purchased by suppliers of Tier-1, Tier-2, Tier-3, and beyond that are used to manufacture components and direct raw material inputs supplied to a channel master. Figure 3.3 depicts the purchase of aluminum across the supply chain.

Large firms that use large volumes are able to negotiate the most favorable terms and conditions for their bulk purchases of raw materials, such as aluminum. In many cases, the channel master is the largest link in the supply chain. The difference in terms of price and quality of raw material becomes apparent as one traverses down a supply chain to Tier-2 and Tier-3 suppliers. The smaller tier suppliers, purchasing lower volumes of aluminum, usually pay higher prices than the channel master for the raw material, often from the same aluminum producer. Yet these higher prices paid by the smaller tier suppliers are still reflected in the cost of the end product for the channel master.

An obvious strategy for realizing substantial savings across the supply chain is to collectively negotiate the purchase of aluminum for the entire supply chain. This will ensure that the smaller tier suppliers not only get the same price breaks as the channel master, but also get preferential treatment for delivery. The larger consolidated volume may even prompt further price breaks. To make this work, the channel master has to take the leadership role in identifying potential raw materials or services for pooling across the supply chain. This requires a careful study of the finished product, and value-add processes, at every stage of the productive process of a tier supplier. The basis for a cost-benefit analysis is identifying common content across the supply chain, the prices paid by each supplier for that content, and the potential savings that would be realized from aggregating that buy. A proposed technology and process solution to enable the purchase of indirect raw materials is entirely dependent on the agreements crafted between the trading partners and the channel master.

Pooling indirect raw materials purchases across the supply chain has the potential for making a significant impact on the invisible costs across the supply chain. The challenge for the channel master is to ensure that the cost savings from the purchase of pooled raw material are reflected in the prices charged between the trading partners. Successful implementation of a buying consortium requires demonstrable cost savings for the trading partners and the channel master. These savings have to be greater than the costs of administering the transactions. Any technology and process solutions must include a mechanism to audit the transfer pricing and ensure that savings from lower prices are being passed to the channel master.

This idea of purchasing consortiums across the supply chain is not new. However, past efforts in this area have not been successful due to the cost of coordination across multiple firms. With affordable Internet technologies, it is feasible to coordinate these activities in a cost-efficient manner. The Center for Advanced Purchasing Studies highlights the following critical success factors for this approach:

1. Trading partners involved in the indirect raw materials program, across the supply chain should share equitably in the costs, risks, and rewards from such a venture. More often than not, the channel master dictates the terms and conditions for participating in a buying consortium to the trading partners. The channel master rarely explains benefits of participating in such an endeavor and the costs and risks of implementing the processes are pushed to the suppliers. Getting a shared frame of reference to the costs, risks, and rewards across the supply chain is essential to success of the buying consortium.

2. The relationship among the trading partners should be based on trust and cooperation. To accomplish the preceding objective necessitates more than an arm's-length relationship among the trading partners. This is very difficult to achieve and sustain for long periods of time. Clearly articulated areas of trust and cooperation as they relate to achieving the buying consortiums objectives, without breaking any anti-trust laws, will simplify the process.

3. It should be cost-beneficial to all trading partners to participate in the program. It may transpire that some trading partners may want to opt out of the consortium if it does not align with that particular firm's financial and strategic objectives. In such a case, the channel master mandating participation in the consortium through implicit or explicit methods can lead to undesirable consequences for the consortium.

4. Channel partners should ensure that no anti-trust laws are violated. There are strict laws governing pooling buying power across multiple firms to drive down prices. The channel master and trading partners should refer to the prevailing legal rulings on buying consortia.

5. Information relating to transactions should be secured and not available to competitors.[3]

In subsequent chapters we will discuss specific process and technology issues associated with the product categories that make up the traditional supply chain in a market economy, especially direct raw materials and services. But before we proceed, let's revisit some of the product and service categories that offer great potential for cost savings but that are not usually considered part of the traditional supply chain, namely MRO and PPE. Recall the difficulties John Requisitioner had in trying to purchase static wipes for his office computer. Let's find out how to help him. We will now look at various subcategories in the MRO area and recommend some strategies for reducing costs.

Maintenance, Repair, and Operations Cost Savings

Low Risk, Low Value

Cost savings for this category of MRO products and services are the easiest to implement. The static wipes example earlier in the chapter illustrates this category. As the case study reveals, typical costs in this area arise from the administrative tasks associated with identifying a product, qualifying suppliers, authorization, receiving, and payment processes. Given the low-value nature of this category, examining the supply chain for additional cost savings (as we did in the case of indirect raw materials) offers little or no incremental benefit. All the avoidable costs are a result of the transaction process itself.

The goals of a procurement process to reduce the avoidable costs for this category are as follows:

- Simplify procedures to order a product or service in this category, for example by using catalogs (online or offline).

- Make the approval process easy to follow and transparent. This will reduce the amount of unnecessary follow-up activities by the requisitioner.

- Enforce control through process, for example, via automation. Avoid manual intervention. Low-dollar-value items should not need multiple signatures to release the purchase order.

---

[3] Thomas Hendrick, "Purchasing Consortiums: Horizontal Alliances among Firms Buying Common Goods and Services. What? Who? Why? How?" Center for Advanced Purchasing Studies Focus Study, 1997.

Consider the example of low-value office supplies. Every member of a firm has a dollar limit to which they are authorized to buy supplies for a given budget period. Acquiring office supplies using manual ordering and approval processes adds cost without corresponding value. Automating the approval process allows the purchasing department to do a more thorough job of auditing after the fact as a result of being able to review online purchasing data. For example, consolidating the office products catalog online via a Web interface, and presetting spending limits for various departments and individuals would free the purchasing department to analyze purchasing trends. Firms could then use this analysis to negotiate better prices for higher-dollar-volume commodities.

The key enabling technologies are a combination of electronic catalogs and automated work-flow-based approval tools. Using these technologies allows finance and purchasing departments to focus on negotiating better terms and conditions for commodities rather than on expediting and processing transactions. Note that this approach will not work for other categories, because the characteristics of the category dictate the technology solution options. Let us now turn to another MRO category to illustrate this point.

Low Risk, High Value

Recall from Chapter 2 that office productivity software and computing facilities fall into the category of low-risk, high-value MRO items. Most of these high-value items do not cause a lot of transactions. The same framework suggested for low-risk, low-value MRO items can be used with the following modifications:

- Negotiated prices appear in the catalogs.

- Competitive bidding and auction features are implemented for standard items with multiple substitutes.

- Automated approval processes must be implemented with dollar-limit interventions and alerts.

Because of the high value of the MRO items in this category, prices are usually negotiated. A purchasing specialist is assigned to a particular product category and negotiates price breaks based on volume, advance commitment, etc. Having a specialist in place for certain high-value items allows negotiation for immediate price reduction in case the prices for certain inputs to the MRO item decrease. For example, if the firm buys high-end workstations for its staff, prices can be renegotiated whenever the prices for key inputs—such as microprocessors—fall.

Competitive bidding and auction features remove costs from sourcing standard MRO items with multiple substitutes. A major cost factor here is the manual cost of administering, selecting, and awarding a competitive bid—or conducting an auction. Having automated bidding and/or auction features that are invisible to the requisitioner but open to prequalified suppliers removes the administrative costs and generates considerable savings.

An automated approval process was recommended for low-risk, low-value MRO items. It is also important for the high-value category. Automated approval frees the purchasing function to focus more on auditing and negotiating favorable prices. However, high-value MRO items require proactive alerts to the audit function based on dollar thresholds. A replacement motor costing thousands of dollars may be needed for smooth operations of a factory. The authority to order this part would be delegated to the plant supervisor as necessary. It is feasible that given the high resale value of the replacement motor, an unscrupulous plant supervisor might order unnecessary replacement motors and sell them on the secondary market. Designing an audit process that requires verifying the need for the replacement motor will increase the cycle time in acquiring and installing the replacement motor. A proactive alert to the audit function to verify the transaction after the fact is equally effective and does not impact the ability of the plant supervisor to keep the assembly line rolling.

The low-risk, high-value MRO category is one area in which the costs can be reduced for both the visible transaction component and the invisible price component. Automated approval and catalog systems address transaction costs, competitive bidding, and advance commitment to purchase. The functionality needed from the supporting process and technology solutions must focus on proactively managing the procurement of low-risk, high-value MRO items. It is this proactive commodity management that reduces invisible costs.

High Risk, Low Value

For high-risk, low-value MRO items, the price component is of minimal importance. Unfortunately, most traditional purchasing processes are geared solely toward reducing price. As the following example illustrates, opportunity costs arising from poor quality or lack of reliable supply should be the driving factor in determining the process and technology solutions.

A typical manufacturing plant needs spare parts to keep the production line operational. Getting a price break on 5-cent bolts is not as important as ensuring that the bolts are available when and where the maintenance personnel need them. Many organizations misguidedly reward purchasing personnel who spend an inordinate amount of time locating the cheapest bolts for the firm's maintenance needs. The purchasing organization may have saved thousands of dollars by buying those bolts in large quantities. However, if the bolts are not readily available at the point of need, those cost savings quickly evaporate. Rarely is the cost of maintenance personnel searching for the needed bolts factored in. In such a scenario, it may be more efficient to pay higher prices to have smaller quantities procured, but with the expectation that the supplier will stock the bolts where they are readily available to the maintenance crew.

Similarly, a poor-quality part or lack of a part may force a plant shutdown. Clearly, if there is risk of a shutdown, getting spare parts solely on the basis of price is not cost-efficient. Using a supplier who not only commits to quality but also has a contingency plan to ensure that the plant never halts for want of a spare part may be the cost-beneficial alternative. Opportunity costs are rarely factored into the decision-making process for high-risk, low-value MRO items. Maintenance personnel rarely have a say in the procurement decision-making process. In the "all nuts are not equal" case discussed in Chapter 2, the shop floor personnel were never part of the sourcing decision. They expressed reservations about awarding the contract for nuts to a distant supplier. Their objections were overruled with the explanation that the local vendor had befriended the shop floor personnel. The purchasing function did not see or account for the time spent in searching for MRO items in its buying decision.

There is a trade-off between low prices and invisible costs. These invisible costs that need to be kept in mind are primarily related to idle and wasted resources—personnel and PPE. The catalog and approval processes for the two MRO categories discussed (low-risk, low-value and low-risk, high-value) can be used with the following modifications:

■ Allow the suppliers to interact directly with requisitioners to resolve issues related to the supply and use of the products and services in this category.

- Facilitate supplier management of inventory, availability, usage, and contingency planning.

Allowing the supplier of the product or service to interact with the requisitioner can take many forms. Suppliers may provide technical help in the use of a particular spare part or assist in the proper hiring of qualified contingency staff. The transaction and order approval process can be similar to the other MRO categories with one major exception. The automated approval and release process should not require any manual approvals. Requiring manual approvals has the potential to create a scenario where a critical spare part cannot be obtained for want of a missing person's approval. Auditing should be done using the automated system after the transaction has taken place. An earlier example in this chapter discusses auditing the acquisition of high-value replacement motors. A similar approach is needed for low-value MRO items. Given the relatively low dollar value of the purchases, fraud or theft should not be significant cost factors. The costs of a plant shutdown far outweigh the benefits of theft prevention for a low-dollar-value item by introducing audit and approval processes that add to the MRO procurement cycle time.

The functionality and features of the process and technology solutions to support the high-risk, low-value MRO category must be focused on item availability and supplier support to the requisitioner. In this category collaborative systems that facilitate the interaction between the end user and suppliers will help avoid unnecessary costs.

High Risk, High Value

High-risk, high-value MRO items are generally not procured from a catalog or through a competitive auction process. Engineering equipment, communications systems, and complex ERP software are examples of products and services in this category. Selecting a supplier for this category typically involves a detailed request for proposal (RFP) process. Many of the negotiations between potential suppliers and the procurer are related to the definition of what is required. In-depth market and competitive analysis are also part of the selection process.

To support this activity, the use of collaborative systems that allow suppliers to participate will reduce cycle time and costs associated with coordinating teams across multiple departments. Even after a contract is awarded, the supplier is usually involved in knowledge transfer, training, or similar activities for a considerable period of time. Continued involvement of the supplier in a support and maintenance capacity will be needed in most cases. Coordinated and planned action is essential to minimize costs and risks associated with procuring products and services in this category. Appropriate process and technology infrastructure to support collaboration, project planning, and execution tasks across multiple firms will reduce risks and costs associated with this category.

Property, Plant, and Equipment Procurement Costs

The procurement costs associated with PPE are very similar to those of the high-risk, high-value MRO category. Close collaboration with suppliers is required not only to specify and design what is being procured, but also to optimize the delivery and installation process. Acquiring PPE usually involves large capital investments. To optimize capital utilization, it is essential to put new PPE to use with minimum idle time. All parts, equipment, and labor needed to erect a new plant, for example, need to be available at precisely the right time to minimize the risk of high idle time costs. Costs associated with partially completed PPE waiting for some critical component—because the labor was not scheduled properly or a critical shipment of wiring was delayed—can be substantial. Contingency planning in case of unplanned shortages is essential for cost avoidance in this category.

Collaboration is a challenge, because suppliers in a PPE project can be quite diverse. Consider some of the inputs into a new office complex. The office may need data and fiber-optic cabling to be installed as well as curtain blinds. The high-technology service firm that does cabling may have an entirely different technology infrastructure from the firm installing the blinds. Not surprisingly, coordination of these tasks is outsourced to construction firms. Because of the diversity of PPE suppliers, a collaborative infrastructure that allows multiple firms with varying degrees of technological sophistication to share project plans and update completed tasks is essential to cost minimization. Training to use the infrastructure before commencement of PPE activity is also mandatory to minimize costs.

Maintenance, Repair, and Operations and Outsourced Services

An alternative to developing the infrastructure and systems to procure MRO–ype items is to outsource that function to an integrated MRO supplier. A typical Fortune 500 firm has thousands of suppliers, and a significant number of those suppliers fall into the MRO category. Managing each and every supplier relationship places a heavy burden on a firm's administrative overhead. Contracting with an integrated MRO supplier allows a firm to reduce the number of individual MRO suppliers.

For example, the integrated MRO supplier acts as the lead supplier for an area such as lubricants. Instead of dealing with a multitude of MRO suppliers, the purchasing department can now focus on the suppliers of strategic direct raw materials, components, and services. Usually, the integrated MRO supplier focuses exclusively on a particular class of products and services and becomes an expert in their procurement and support.

Other services traditionally performed within firms that have become commoditized are promising candidates for outsourcing. Good examples of these services are payroll processing, benefits administration, and accounts receivable collection. Processes and technologies to support outsourced services are generally long term and need integration and collaboration with the existing processes and systems in a firm. A general-purpose cookie-cutter technology or process solution will not work, as the attributes of outsourced services will differ substantially based on the nature of the service.

A critical element to reducing costs associated with outsourced services is the ability to monitor service level agreements (SLA) and performance guarantees. In most outsourcing scenarios, vendors and firms spend an inordinate amount of time and effort over the life of the contract trying to prove that a service was performed as expected. Avoiding this requires very clearly defined SLAs before the start of the engagement and solutions for monitoring and reporting on the SLAs after the vendor begins to provide the service.

Global Sourcing

In the preceding discussing, much of our focus has been on firms operating domestically. Today, however, entirely domestic operations are the exception, not the rule. Throughout the last 20 years, the imperatives of cost efficiency and customer responsiveness have pushed firms toward global location of production and distribution facilities and time-based competition. Globalization is motivated by pressures to maximize cost efficiencies and economies of scale, as well as the need to obtain access to new markets. It has been facilitated by liberalization of trade policies by governments and freer flow of capital all over the world. Firms are not only outsourcing production and service facilities, they are outsourcing them to partners located around the globe.

At the same time that trading partners are located in ever more remote locations, firms are struggling to respond to customer demands for more customization and speedier fulfillment of orders. Clearly, firms' resources are stretched to respond to these conflicting demands. While outsourcing the manufacture of a component to an Asian plant may be cost-efficient in terms of labor, added coordination and shipping costs must be considered, not to mention the added time required to ship components from Asia to their next destination. We need to systematically examine the visible and invisible costs associated with procuring and distributing products and services globally.

Visible Costs in Global Sourcing

Many of the visible cost categories are analogous to the ones discussed in the domestic context, but addressing them is much more complex. Both for MRO and direct raw materials, the costs of locating a product, placing the order, securing purchase and payment approvals, and receiving also exist in the global context. For many firms with long-time overseas affiliates, activities were not coordinated on a global scale. Although final products were made in one country and then shipped to the different distribution centers around the world, MRO sourcing, for example, was entirely in the decision domain of each local affiliate. A multitude of foreign MRO suppliers was being used by a multitude of foreign affiliates. Therefore, volume discounts could not be negotiated across country borders.

This fragmentation is not unique to MRO. In fact, an executive of a large automotive manufacturer once stated that the only two common parts on the company's globally best-selling small car were the nameplate and the water pump. Everything else was sourced separately in each of the countries in which the car was assembled.

More porous borders, new foreign competitors, and advances in IT have provided new opportunities for achieving cost efficiencies. Increasingly, firms are seeking to consolidate some of their purchases across national borders; in addition, they are establishing regional rather than national manufacturing and distribution facilities.

Although efficiency and economies of scale can be realized, it is important to keep in mind that some of the visible costs discussed above have added components in the global context. Although locating a product anywhere in the world has become much easier using Web technology, comparing features and price, as well as assessing the quality of the potential supplier, are made harder by both geographic and cultural distances. While shipment of goods and services across borders has become cheaper and easier, firms still have to deal with currency fluctuation and differences in legal systems and business cultures around the world. Additional components are introduced into the SCM process, such as import and export agencies, multinational distributors, and customs offices.

Systems that address visible cost components will have to be more complex. A multitude of standardization issues arise. For example, will the decimal separator in the supporting financial systems be the period (as in the United Kingdom and the United States), or will it be a comma (as in continental Europe). When trying to implement the Global Food Exchange, an electronic marketplace that deals in perishable foods, technology turned out to be a major issue. The same food can be known by different names and descriptions in various parts of the world. Technology has to account for these differences and know that aubergine, eggplant, and brinjal are the same vegetable.

In the services industries, much of the data management across borders has to do with personnel files. Here, firms have to recognize the stringent restrictions that some countries place on the cross-border transfer of personal information. This issue is especially pertinent for multinational firms dealing with the European Union (EU). In 1995, the EU implemented its data protection directive, setting standards for the protection of personal data. This directive focuses on protecting the privacy of individuals, and it forbids the transmission of personal data to countries where this data is not protected to the same degree as in EU member states. Because the United States does not have strong legal privacy protection, transfer of personal data from the European countries to the United States could potentially be prohibited. Europeans consider the use of personal data for direct marketing purposes especially objectionable if it is implemented without the knowledge of the targeted individual. Furthermore, employees and consumers have the right to opt out of such marketing campaigns without cost.

The case of Citibank illustrates the point. In 1994, even before the implementation of the latest EU directive, Citibank finalized an agreement with the German railroads to issue their credit cards. But when it was revealed that the credit card information would be processed in the United States instead of in Germany, the German government announced that, in the absence of adequate U.S. privacy standards, the agreement would be prohibited. Multinational firms using expatriate personnel have to be sure to secure permission for data transfers across borders. In the professional sectors, the maintenance of global repositories of data on employee qualifications and skills is made very difficult. System implantations will have to account for differences in data collected and transferred between multinational systems.

Invisible Costs in Global Sourcing

Recall the four categories of invisible costs: dispute resolution, working capital and buffer inventories, unplanned shipping costs, and costs associated with indirect raw materials. Disputes are even more likely to arise in the procurement of goods and services overseas. Legal systems vary, and it may be costly or altogether ineffective to go to court in a foreign country. For high-volume transactions, for example, for MRO–type commodity items, standardization of processes is also desirable in the global context; however, it is much harder to implement. For customized inputs, such as components, the dispute resolution process needs to be clearly laid out before any transactions occur. A cost-benefit analysis of global sourcing must include an assessment of the consequences of nonfulfillment by an overseas supplier. In some instances, this assessment must include writing off the disputed purchase entirely.

For direct raw materials, the global environment aggravates costs arising from working capital, buffer inventory, and unplanned shipping. Recall that these costs were attributed to communication problems between the firm and the multiple tiers of its suppliers. Obviously, communication is harder across different languages, different cultures, and different time zones. Much of the routine information exchange needs to be formalized and automated a priori to avoid misunderstandings. The channel master has to provide adequate planning information to the suppliers. In return, the suppliers reduce buffer inventories and pass on the cost savings to the channel master. The supplier relationship becomes defined by mutual trust. Development of trust is also harder across cultures.

For indirect raw materials, purchases can be pooled across the supply chain to achieve greater economies of scale. For commodity-type inputs, this is also an option for globally operating firms. Most suppliers of commodities operate on a global scale; therefore, they can follow their customers wherever their services and products are needed. Recall the global automotive example, where only the nameplate and the water pump were common to the final product. The nameplate was manufactured in-house in only one location, and it was a common part to many more models. The water pump was common to all final products because the supplier was a global firm and sold the same product worldwide.

In the global environment, pooling of raw materials, components, and services procurement also has added costs. The benefits of price breaks due to larger purchase volumes have to be weighed against added transportation and coordination costs. Internet technologies make global pooling of indirect raw materials purchases possible. But, as with the other cost categories, implementation is made harder by legal and cultural differences. In addition, technological sophistication and the willingness to conduct business using these technologies can vary widely across countries.

Multiple Approaches to Cost Avoidance

There are multiple approaches to reducing both the visible and invisible costs associated with the purchase of goods and services by a firm. Generally, cost reductions that can contribute the most to a firm's bottom line are not readily apparent. These costs occur primarily in the area of direct and indirect raw materials purchase and require a detailed study of the productive processes across the trading partner firms of a supply chain.

Visible costs, however, can be more easily addressed. Visible costs occur primarily in the area of transaction processing. The category that generates the largest number of transactions is that of MRO products and services. Implementation of automated Web-based ordering systems, coupled with work-flow and approval systems, can immediately impact the bottom line.

Alternatively, some or all of the transaction processing can be outsourced to integrated suppliers. In addition to reducing the visible and invisible cost factors discussed in this chapter, the approaches outlined can have the following benefits:

- Reduce the cycle time involved in identifying and procuring a good or service.

- Create the infrastructure for strategic relationships with key suppliers.

- Develop a clear audit trail with the use of automated centralized systems.

- Allow visibility of the various goods and services procured across the enterprise. This puts the buying firm back in control of the purchasing process.

- Improve internal customer satisfaction with speed, responsiveness, and transparency of the procurement process.

In sum, processes and technology solutions can be categorized into intermediation technologies and disintermediation technologies. With disintermediation, removal of the intermediate suppliers reduces associated administrative overhead involved in completing a transaction. Most visible costs can be reduced using disintermediation. However, cost savings associated with transaction processing are not as significant as those that can be obtained by addressing the invisible costs in the procurement of direct and indirect raw materials. In these areas, process and technology solutions provide intermediation, and technology takes on the role of process enabler. Intermediation provides collaborative processes and supporting technologies. Collaboration with suppliers has the potential for greater impact on a firm's profits than disintermediation.

Over the years, traditional supply chain system technology solutions have focused on synchronized activities aimed at efficient flow of raw materials and finished products, and optimum utilization of productive assets—within the firm and across the supply chain. The remaining chapters focus on the productive processes and their direct inputs.

Market Economy Solutions

Let's revisit the iceberg analogy introduced in Chapter 3. In Chapters 2 and 3 we saw that direct raw materials and services account for the largest dollar volume of the purchases of a firm. If all the costs within the firm and its supply chain are depicted as an iceberg, as in Figure 4.1, the visible tip can be associated primarily with transaction-processing elements connected with the purchase of high-volume, low-value commodity and operating resources. The larger invisible dollar volume just below the surface represents some of the purchasing costs associated with the procurement of direct raw materials and services.

Expanding on the distinction introduced in Chapter 3, the invisible costs can be separated into two categories. In Figure 4.1, the invisible costs immediately below the water level are associated with transaction-processing activity related to procurement of direct raw materials, services, and efficient utilization of PPE. We used the term market economy model to describe a vertically integrated firm and its supply chain synchronized for optimal utilization of resources across the supply chain. The market economy model is geared toward "pushing" product to the customer based on forecasted market demand. We will use the term *push model* to describe this type of firm and its supporting supply chain. Push model solutions, comprised of process and technologies, target this segment of the invisible costs associated with process efficiencies across the supply chain. Further below the surface lies an even larger portion of the hidden costs, and these are not

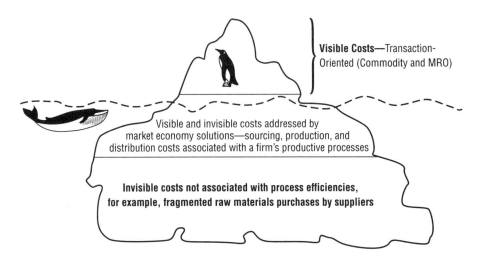

Visible Costs—Transaction-Oriented (Commodity and MRO)

Visible and invisible costs addressed by market economy solutions—sourcing, production, and distribution costs associated with a firm's productive processes

Invisible costs not associated with process efficiencies, for example, fragmented raw materials purchases by suppliers

Figure 4.1: Hidden costs addressed by a push model solution.

associated with process efficiencies. An example of such a hidden cost is the cost embedded in the indirect raw materials purchased by the multiple tiers of the supplier firms.

In this chapter we will discuss SCM solutions aimed at achieving the optimum utilization of physical assets through process efficiencies. The SCM solution supports these process efficiencies within the firm and across the supply chain. The next chapter introduces SCM solutions geared toward optimum utilization of the customer knowledge assets of the firm.

Supply Chain Management Systems Supporting the Push Model

Push model solutions are designed to produce goods and services efficiently to meet forecasted demand; their entire focus is on supporting a tightly integrated enterprise geared toward mass production of goods at the lowest possible price. The productive processes across the supply chain are synchronized for efficient utilization of all resources (capital, PPE, and human resources). Information technology acts as an enabler for operational optimization within the firm and across the supply chain. Technology solutions are geared toward generating better forecasts and synchronizing the sourcing, production, and distribution processes within the firm and across the supply chain to match the forecast.

Let us first briefly outline what SCM means. Figure 4.2 shows the major processes embedded within a push solution.

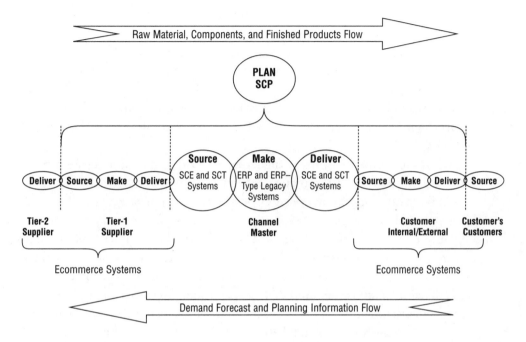

Figure 4.2: Synchronization of a market push solution.

The channel master's plan for a given time period dictates the following activities:

■ Sourcing and staging of raw materials and components

■ Manufacture and assembly of products

■ Distribution of finished products to the customers

The plan is generated by the SCP module, which takes input from historical transaction files and sales and marketing systems among other internal and external sources. The plan generates a demand forecast for the channel master's products. Several different methods of forecasting are discussed in subsequent sections of this chapter. Based on the forecast for the planning period (quarter, month, etc.), the SCP component prepares a detailed breakdown of how the product is going be manufactured and sourced to meet the targets in the forecast. Product specifics from a product development management (PDM) system are used in developing detailed sourcing and manufacturing plans. The specifics on materials needed to manufacture the product and dependencies among the materials are captured in a document called bill of materials (BOM).

The BOM depicts the components in a manner that reflects the manufacturing process. Consider the manufacture of a traditional bed. At a high level, the materials needed to manufacture the bed are a headboard, mattress frame, sideboards, and legs. The BOM at the highest level of planning may reflect these components. The BOM for the headboard specifies materials needed to manufacture one headboard, for example, 30 type x screws, y units of glue, and so on.

The SCP module will use a higher-level BOM and communicate a plan for implementation of the materials requirements planning (MRP) system. (MRP–type systems fall in the supply chain transaction category). The MRP system can blow up the BOM to the desired detail for sourcing and manufacture to meet the plan's targets. Trading partners of the channel master (tier suppliers, transportation providers, etc.) participate with the channel master in setting up procurement, manufacturing, and distribution channels to efficiently manufacture and deliver the product to the customer. The SCP component shown in Figure 4.2 schedules and synchronizes internal production systems for operational efficiency to meet plan objectives. The operational model in Figure 4.2 is an interpretation of the supply chain operations reference (SCOR) model published by the Supply Chain Council (SCC), a nonprofit organization interested in advancing leading-edge SCM systems and practices.

Supply chain execution (SCE) systems primarily aim at reducing the shipping and inventory holding costs across the trading partners and the channel master. Supply chain execution systems provide warehouse and transportation management functionality. The objective of SCE systems is to minimize the holding of raw materials, components, or finished products for the channel master or any trading partners during the value-add process. Trade-offs between shipping, inventory holding costs, and safety inventories determine the holding period of raw materials, components, and finished goods across the supply chain. Systems of the SCP, SCE, and ERP types have built-in best practices to plan and execute to these multiple constraints.

Finally, SCT systems record the transaction information occurring across the supply chain, including the firm and customers; SCT systems are integrated ERP or legacy systems providing functionality spanning the following areas:

- Materials requirements planning
- Production planning and scheduling
- Capacity management
- Inventory management
- Integrated sales, marketing, financial, and human resources management

In light of recent developments in Web technology and the associated proliferation of "e everything," it is important to draw a distinction between two currently popular and often misused terms: ebusiness and ecommerce. Ebusiness systems comprise the entire range of activities depicted in Figure 4.2. A firm engaged in ebusiness not only electronically integrates all internal departments, but it also integrates its suppliers and customers, using Internet, voice response, electronic data interchange (EDI), and similar technologies. In contrast, ecommerce systems focus on the subset of ebusiness functionality that is outward-facing and touches suppliers and customers. In a traditional market economy firm, there is a very tight firewall built around functional systems within a firm. In Figure 4.2, this firewall is shown by dotted lines. The distinction between ecommerce and ebusiness is important to keep in mind, because we will revisit this issue when discussing network economy solutions in the next chapter.

Service Chains

A firm and its supporting trading partner network that provide services exclusively can be termed a *service chain*. This is analogous to the supply chain whose primary focus is on the manufacture and distribution of physical goods. Most service chains—covering areas such as financial services, health care, and contingent staffing—require collaboration among the trading partners for effective and efficient delivery of services. The emphasis here is on sharing the knowledge as it relates to service delivery with all trading partners involved in the production and delivery of the service. Services by their very nature have the scope for a lot more customization than physical products. The process, organization, and technology infrastructure to support this model is much closer to the network economy model (see Chapter 5).

What Supply Chain Management Systems
Can and Can't Do

A recent study conducted at Georgia Tech reported that of 861 firms surveyed, most were unable to document any return on investment (ROI) from SCM technologies. Further, the study states that much of the evidence for ROI is anecdotal, and managers are under pressure to make significant SCM technology decisions with scant analytical data to help them. Our suggested approach for SCM technology selection and implementation puts the business drivers at the forefront. One reason analytical data may be difficult to obtain is the confusion about what benefits to measure from an SCM technology deployment. This confusion has been exacerbated over the years as many ERP vendors have claimed to give a firm the same benefits derived from SCM implementations.

Enterprise resource planning systems provide a high degree of integration among various functions across the enterprise. The accuracy and speed of transactions is significantly improved within the firm. They do not, however, help management in making decisions regarding what products to make or how to source and deliver them based on demand signals from direct and indirect channels. Supply chain management systems, on the other hand, provide decision support capability to managers by allowing what-if analysis to meet various objectives—such as profit or market share. For SCM to deliver on its decision support capabilities, however, requires a good transaction system in place—such as an ERP system. Without one, the SCM system may generate a good plan, but the firm will lack the ability to execute it effectively within the firm and across the supply chain. The transaction systems in turn provide feedback based on actual outcomes (sales and production) to the SCM tools, which incorporate the actual outcomes and regenerate the strategic and tactical actual plans. Supply chain management functionality can be thought of as a modeling and simulation decision support system that determines the optimum plan based on various constraints—production capacity, transportation, and profit goals, among others.

Specific Benefits from Supply Chain
Management Technologies

Before examining the features and functionality of SCM technology solutions, it is necessary to discuss the benefits of SCM for a traditional market economy firm. Table 4.1 lists some of the important benefits for a firm (channel master) and its trading partners. A major business driver for implementing SCM technology is reduction in cash-to-cash cycle time, which is the number of days between the payment for raw materials and other inputs and the receipt of the proceeds from the sale of the finished product or service.

Table 4.1 Some Representative Benefits to a Firm and Its Trading Partners from a Push Solution

Within the Firm	Trading Partners
■ Cash-to-cash cycle time reduction	■ Reduced safety stock
■ Increased inventory turns— efficient use of PPE	■ Lead time to plan raw materials acquisition
■ Transaction cost reductions through integrated processes	■ Reduced administrative and transaction costs
■ Reduced operations and logistics costs	
■ Improved quality—delivery and fill rates	
■ Reduced supply chain coordination costs	

Historically, firms have tried to optimize their cash position by delaying payments and hurrying receipt of incoming cash. Unfortunately, this practice leads to the delayed payment costs of the tier suppliers being passed along into the cost of the finished product. Note that these costs cannot be easily isolated and cannot be attributed to conscious strategic decision making. Rather, this practice is entirely based on actions taken in the accounts receivable and accounts payable departments in an effort to optimize their cash positions. Cost effects are amplified, because both opportunity costs and the interest payments for working capital loans must be factored in.

Supply chain management reduces the cash-to-cash cycle time through efficient ordering, production, and demand fulfillment processes. Supply chain management technology coordinates the flow of raw materials, components, and finished products across the firm's productive process in an efficient manner to minimize the time spent by these materials in non-value-added activities. However, to realize the cost saving in reduced cash-to-cash cycle time, demand forecasts have to be accurate and the products have to be sold as soon as possible after manufacture.

Minimizing cash-to-cash cycle time is a broad approach to process improvement with added benefits. For example, to obtain the best cash-to-cash cycle time requires that the suppliers receive the correct raw materials and component order information with accurate delivery schedules. This information has to be received with enough lead time to allow the suppliers to procure raw materials that meet the quality requirements of the channel master. This timely sharing of information ensures that the productive and distribution processes of the channel master do not suffer from lack of quality inputs to the production processes of the suppliers. Firms that have implemented SCM technology solutions have typically reduced their cash-to-cash cycle time from a median of 100 days to 30 days or less.[1]

A by-product of reducing cash-to-cash cycle times is a potential increase in inventory turns. Higher inventory turns means that the firm's working capital is not tied up in raw materials and components sitting in warehouses. The firm is holding just enough inventory, including safety stock, for its immediate production needs. Determining the optimal level of inventory to hold given warehouse, shipping, ordering, and working capital cost constraints is done very well by most SCM solutions. A firm implementing an SCM technology solution can realize inventory reductions ranging from 25 to 60 percent.[2]

Increased inventory turns, realized through SCM functionality, positively impact the utilization of a firm's PPE. The productive process within the firm is orchestrated by SCM systems to realize maximum utilization of PPE and human resources through effective raw materials sourcing, production scheduling, and capacity and distribution management. To achieve this objective, SCM requires tightly integrated processes within the firm, its suppliers, and distribution channels. This tight integration allows the optimization of transactional, administrative, operational, and supply chain coordination costs. A few representative tangible benefits for best-in-class integrated supply chain firms are:

- Reduced material acquisition costs as a percent of total acquisition costs from 3.2 percent to 2.2 percent.

---

[1] "Supply Chain Management–Benchmarks," *CIO Magazine,* Oct. 21, 2000, p. 110.

[2] Supply Chain Council, PRTM ISC Benchmark Survey, 1997.

- Compressed sourcing cycle times from 90 days to 1 day.

- Compressed production cycle time from 30 days to 3 days.

- Reduced work-in-process inventory from 25 days to 17 days.

- Lowered order management costs as a percent of total ordering costs from 11.3 percent to 9.3 percent.[3]

Formal process definition and tight adherence to the process are required to synchronize the efficient flow of raw materials, components, and finished goods from the suppliers to the firm and the distribution channels. Having a visible process offers further opportunities for continued process improvement leading to additional cost reductions and operating efficiencies.

Such tight integration with suppliers has the added benefit of being able to improve quality. The coordination required by implementing SCM systems and associated processes provides the legitimacy and incentives for channel master firms to go upstream in the supply chain to detect and rectify any raw materials quality problems. Improved quality obviously results in reduced warranty costs.

As a result of production planning and scheduling information being communicated across the supply chain, operating and logistics costs are reduced for the firm and its trading partners. For example, the lead times built into SCM systems mean that suppliers receive timely information on when and where to stage the raw materials in the productive processes of their customers, enabling the suppliers to negotiate for reduced rates for their raw materials, transportation, warehouse, and other productive resources. This can significantly reduce the costs associated with receiving, unpacking, and staging the raw materials for production. The staging of materials and components by the suppliers also avoids the costs of storage in warehouses because the inputs are put immediately into production.

Finally, new product design or production changes can be communicated through SCM functionality, allowing for the smooth transition from one product to a different product without disrupting the supply chain. Coordinating product changes efficiently across the supply chain reduces wastage from obsolescence of materials and components for the firm and its trading partners.

---

[3] Supply Chain Council Benchmark Survey.

Critical Success Factors for Realizing Benefits from a Push Solution

Supply chain systems for the market economy are designed to serve the push model of product flow. Recall that this model requires accurate forecasting and information exchange. In most systems, this information exchange takes place in the form of production and delivery plans, schedules, material specifications, and staging information. Efficient movement of raw materials, components, and finished products across the supply chain is the goal. Trading partners benefit by being able to plan their own sourcing, manufacturing, and delivery in a deliberate manner. Cost saving are accrued by speeding up the productive processes and by reducing unnecessary buffer inventories across the supply chain.

What happens if forecasts, schedules, and plans are either inaccurate or not relayed in a timely manner? In such cases, costs can rise dramatically. In the worst-case scenario, the entire productive process throughout the supply chain is halted because components or raw materials are not available when needed. Alternatively, if the decision is made to quickly find other sources for materials or components, the result will be increased costs due to unscheduled shipping and unfavorable pricing.

However, the critical success factor allowing trading partners to benefit from an SCM solution is not just availability to production plans of the channel master, but also *timely and stable* availability. Processes and incentive structures have to be aligned to support the push technology. Consider the example of a sales staff that is compensated by meeting quarterly sales objectives. Toward the end of a quarter, they will have the incentive to push product into the indirect channels to meet their sales quotas. This has the effect of negating the efforts of the entire SCM effort. Upstream suppliers may ignore the demand signals coming from the supplier, believing that they are caused by sales groups trying to meet their quotas for sales commission. If production plans change frequently or are affected by the sales staff trying to meet quotas, the entire supply chain can be disrupted. The lack of sufficient lead time for the suppliers to plan sourcing, manufacture, and delivery activities has what is known as a "bullwhip effect," magnifying the changes throughout the supply chain. For example, frequent increases or decreases in demand may lead to disproportional changes in raw materials availability in the supply chain. The further upstream a supplier is from a channel master, the larger the perturbation.

It is important to underscore that deploying SCM technology does not guarantee the business benefits outlined earlier. Realizing full business benefits from an SCM implementation will depend on the accuracy of the demand forecast for a given time period—assuming no raw material shortage or other problems with the supply chain. Now that we have understood the potential benefits of a push solution, let us look at the functionality provided by various components of the SCM solution framework.

Supply Chain Management Solution Framework

As discussed previously, SCM technologies can be categorized into three areas: SCP, SCE, and SCT. These categories may develop subcategories as the supporting technologies evolve. Supply chain planning sits at the top of the SCM pyramid. The planning component allows the evaluation of various what-if scenarios on sourcing, distribution, and manufacturing decisions without committing the plans for execution. Once a plan is committed to, the execution component sources the materials and PPE to manufacture to the plan. The transaction component records all transactions that occur within the firm and across the supply chain in manufacturing to the plan. Some planning systems have a feedback mechanism through which they recast plans based on actual sourcing, distribution, and manufacturing outcomes—for a variety of reasons; there will be deviations from plan.

Supply Chain Planning

Supply chain planning is at the heart of most SCM solutions. Supply chain planning systems are often compared to ERP systems. Because managers frequently get confused between the functionality offered by ERP–type systems and the functionality offered by SCP, we must first put ERP–type legacy system functionality in perspective.

Enterprise resource planning–type systems are primarily focused on enabling high-volume, reliable, and integrated transactions within the firm, such as fulfilling customer orders, scheduling productive resources (PPE and human), and integrating sales, marketing, financial, and human resources functions. They were designed to break functional silos within a firm, allowing different functional systems to have the same view of a transaction. Their primary task is to optimize all activities in a coordinated manner for efficient production of finished products. Thus ERP systems can be viewed as highly reliable transaction systems with accurate data on work-in-process inventory, production schedules, materials resource planning breakdowns, etc. In contrast, SCP is outward-looking, addressing the flow of materials and components in and out of the firm and supporting sourcing, manufacture, and delivery to forecasted demand.

Enterprise resource planning–type systems have accurate data on the quantity and availability of raw materials and components at every production facility within the firm. Supply chain planning systems use that information on a continual basis to evaluate the ability of the firm to meet forecasted demand for a given product. In case of unforeseen changes or problems, SCP systems incorporate factors such as supplier lead time and transportation and warehouse costs to generate a sourcing plan to get back on track. In contrast to SCP systems, ERP systems do not have the full functionality to plan across the supply chain; they are, however, necessary to realize the full benefits from an SCM implementation.

Figure 4.3 shows the major components of an SCP solution. Supply chain planning functionality can be broken down along strategic and tactical dimensions. Strategic components focus on long-term planning for setting up sourcing strategies and building infrastructure (PPE) for cost-efficient acquisition of raw materials, staging for production, and distribution of finished products. Tactical SCP components focus on coordinating raw materials flows to meet near-term and immediate production needs. In Figure 4.3 the strategic planning components at the top are converted into weekly and daily action plans in the boxes.

The coordinated actions of all trading partners in the supply chain are best represented by a musical analogy. The planning component can be thought of as the sheet music for a symphony. Every musician receives the sheet music ahead of time, which shows where his or her instrument plays and for exactly how long. If the musician botches the cue on when to start and when to stop playing, it can have a ripple effect on the quality of the performance of the entire musical piece. Similarly, attention to timing and execution is critical to realizing the goals of SCM systems.

Like the sheet music, SCP provides top-down control to all trading partners to minimize the variability of outcomes. Historically, business process reengineering projects have failed because there was little or no linkage between the strategic and tactical action plans. In SCP systems, the link between the strategic and daily action plans is very tightly coordinated.

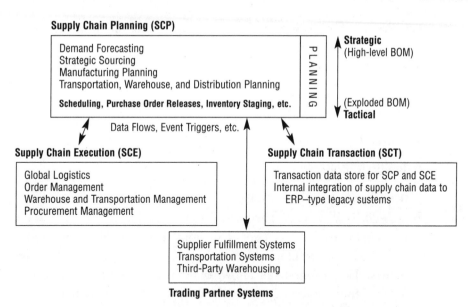

Supply Chain Planning (SCP)

Demand Forecasting
Strategic Sourcing
Manufacturing Planning
Transportation, Warehouse, and Distribution Planning

Scheduling, Purchase Order Releases, Inventory Staging, etc.

P L A N N I N G

▲ **Strategic**
↑ (High-level BOM)

(Exploded BOM)
▼ **Tactical**

Data Flows, Event Triggers, etc.

Supply Chain Execution (SCE)

Global Logistics
Order Management
Warehouse and Transportation Management
Procurement Management

Supply Chain Transaction (SCT)

Transaction data store for SCP and SCE
Internal integration of supply chain data to
ERP–type legacy sustems

Supplier Fulfillment Systems
Transportation Systems
Third-Party Warehousing

Trading Partner Systems

Figure 4.3: Functional components of a push technology solution.

The strategic and tactical plans are based on expected conditions, such as demand forecasts, production capacity, availability and prices of raw materials and components, and human resources. The ability to forecast expected conditions accurately becomes a critical success factor in realizing the business objectives listed in Table 4.1. To account for possible changes and to gather necessary information for future planning periods, information flows continually between the major components of the SCM planning module. The data flows shown in Figure 4.3 illustrate that the SCP module does not just generate static plans for a period. Supply chain planning is an iterative planning process that modifies tactical action plans based on feedback from operational systems. However, even if the firm is able to produce most efficiently to projected demands, it will fail to meet its cash-to-cash objective if the finished products are not sold. A core component of SCP is demand forecasting, which helps a firm determine expected demand for its product for a future period.

Demand Forecasting

Demand forecasting is at the heart of synchronizing SCP activities within the organization and across the trading partners. To use the symphony analogy, demand forecasting can be viewed as writing the musical score for the entire supply chain for a planning period. Most SCP technology solutions have demand forecasting techniques that are derived from industry best practices. Three major categories are:

- Time-series forecasting

- Causal forecasting

- Predictive forecasting

Time-series forecasting relies on historical transaction data from ERP–type and legacy systems. The historical data used for these types of forecasts may go back over many years or may just cover the previous week. There are numerous statistical techniques to choose from to generate time-series forecasts. They range from allowing for trends and seasonal variation to weighing and combining other historical data. These methods discern patterns in historical data and extrapolate to generate product demand forecasts.

Causal forecasting incorporates pertinent economic indicators such as housing starts, inflation, and new goods orders that may impact the demand for a firm's product. Using causal forecasting, sophisticated econometric models can be built and used to generate demand forecasts. In some instances, SCP systems may need to be coupled with sophisticated statistical analysis applications to run these models effectively. Note that access to high-quality, reliable, historical transaction data is necessary to use these forecasting techniques. Inaccurate data will lead to invalid or wildly inaccurate forecasts. Obviously, selecting the wrong forecasting model with accurate historical data may have the same effect. Finally, predictive methods are based on a combination of market and expert surveys, and on extrapolating demand from experience with similar products. To some degree, predictive methods are based on the intuition of experts. This intuition may run from a gut feeling of the market experts to detailed historical information gained from similar products.

Every decision a manager makes regarding sourcing, making, and distributing a product is determined by the expected demand for a given period. For example, hiring direct labor, building fabrication and assembly lines, and setting up distribution channels for shipping products are all activities triggered by the forecast. However, in addition to the forecast, all stars have to align perfectly for optimal results. Only an accurate forecast, an efficient supply chain, and operationally excellent production facilities coupled with superb distribution channels will allow a firm to realize all the benefits from SCM depicted in Figure 4.2. Integrated SCP functionality is available from traditional ERP software packages from vendors such as SAP, Oracle, and PeopleSoft. There are other vendors, such as Manugistics and I2, whose sole focus is SCP.

Supply Chain Execution Systems

Supply chain execution systems provide the functionality to physically manage the procurement, storing, and staging of raw materials, intermediate components, and finished goods throughout the supply chain plan. The SCP module plans the optimum way to procure, make, and distribute finished goods to meet the demand forecast. Supply chain execution systems manage the actual flow of goods and services to achieve the plan objectives. Traditional ERP vendor applications such as SAP and Oracle provide limited SCE functionality. Other vendors in this area focus on specialized functions, from warehouse management to electronic procurement. Some of the software technology vendors serving this part of the spectrum are Descartes, Provia, Arriba, and Commerce One.

Supply Chain Transaction Systems

Supply chain transaction systems have a broad range of functionality. Such systems are primarily systems of record. The range of functionality covers sales orders, inventory management, historical data warehouses, and operational data stores such as point-of-sale systems. The most commonly known SCT systems are probably manufacturing systems such as MRP systems, which use forecasted demand for a given period to manage inventories and control the production lot sizes. The goal of MRP is to avoid inventory shortages and ensure that production runs smoothly according to the manufacturing firm's plans—that is, to produce products to meet forecasted demand. The financial objectives are to reduce the firm's investment in raw materials and work-in-process inventories.

Note, however, that again these objectives are inward-looking and do not take the entire supply chain into consideration. Supply chain planning systems take data from MRP and other legacy data stores to generate a demand forecast and sourcing plan that provides operational efficiencies across the entire supply chain, not just the manufacturing firm. Manufacturing resource planning–type and enterprise resource planning–type systems within a firm integrate and coordinate the activities of manufacturing, engineering, sales and marketing, finance, and other internal functional departments. These MRP– and ERP–type systems store data about all events in the sourcing, production, and delivery cycle, and they act as the integrator for SCP systems. Representative examples of software vendors in this category are Oracle, SAP, PeopleSoft, JD Edwards, and Baan. In addition, many firms have internally developed custom legacy systems that provide functionality in billing, accounts receivable, production, sales order management, and other areas.

Limitations of Push Technology Solutions

Despite software vendor claims to the contrary, it is difficult to have a customer-focused supply technology solution that is operationally efficient. The limitations stem from the contradictory nature of these goals. There are, of course, a few firms that claim to be customer-focused and also operationally able to produce high-quality, customized products at the lowest cost. Despite such claims, the goals of being the lowest-cost producer and producing highly customizable and customer-focused products within the same firm are inherently incompatible.

Providing highly customized products and superior customer service requires that a firm's systems (people, processes, and technology) be customer-focused. Conversely, to be the lowest-cost and operationally superior firm dictates that the firm's systems be focused on sourcing, making, and delivering product to the customer at the lowest possible cost. This is not to say that an operationally superior manufacturing firm lacks flexibility. According to the 1997 SCC Benchmark Survey, best-in-class firms utilizing SCP systems were able to attain up to 65 percent production flexibility. However, that same study found that the delivery performance to customer requests improved by only 1 percent.[4] This finding should not be a surprise, since we have clearly shown how the aggregate demand for a *future period* orchestrates the production processes across the supply chain.

---

[4] Supply Chain Council, PRTM ISC Benchmark Survey, 1997.

There is not much room in this tightly synchronized system to produce to order or build to order. In such a scenario, an increase in the customizable attributes of a product will result in a corresponding increase in the number of customizable components and raw materials that have to be stored upstream. The plans generated by an SCP module are dependent on the upstream suppliers' availability to promise (ATP). Availability to promise functionality ensures that a firm can source the required raw materials, schedule production, and meet the planned delivery commitments made to a customer. Changes in ATP status within the firm and across the supply chain are constantly monitored and operational plans redrawn to account for these changes. The Tier-1 suppliers in turn have their processes optimized to meet the forecasted demand of the channel master. The Tier-1 suppliers similarly have their own constraints in areas such as lead times from their suppliers and limited production capacity and flexibility. All these factors, in addition to sourcing from alternative suppliers, are incorporated in ATP functionality.

The master plan generated by the SCP takes into account all these constraints to generate tactical production plans. These plans are constantly optimized and revised based on feedback from operational systems. Thus from an operational perspective, this planning is top-down and bottom-up. This synchronization places the following limits on a firm:

- Locked-in process across the supply chain

- Competitive agility and flexibility limited to the current and related product lines

Processes, people, and systems have to be synchronized across the supply chain for operational optimization. This necessitates processes and technologies that are specific to each task. Changing an optimized process is difficult, because it creates not only locked-in process but also, given the lead time required to implement such synchronized and coordinated systems, reduced competitive agility and flexibility. A process is said to be locked in or not depending on the degree of difficulty involved in switching processes and technology. If it is easy for the firm and supply chain to switch to a different process and system, it can be inferred that neither the process nor the system is locked in. To set up a synchronized process with support from underlying technology creates a locking-in effect that makes change difficult. Recall the bullwhip effect discussed previously. Inaccurate demand forecasts can lead to a bullwhip effect across the supply chain, leading to understocking or overstocking of raw materials, components, and finished goods.

Despite successful implementation of SCM systems, realizing demonstrable business benefits has been an elusive goal. A recent study from Georgia Tech on the relationship between a firm's supply chain system failures and the stock price revealed that, on average, a firm lost anywhere between 9 and 20 percent of its value over a 6-month period. This study also states that most evidence of ROI from supply chain systems is anecdotal at best. A firm with supply chain problems suffered loss in value, irrespective of who was to blame—supply chain partners, software, or other factors. Some major factors that militate against successful SCM system realization are unsound pricing and promotion policies. For example, frequent markdowns and sales to move product from distribution channels wreck havoc on the supply chains. The demand signals fed into the SCP systems from clearance sales and price markdowns not only train customers to wait for such events before buying, but also compound the overstocking problem by triggering a supply chain reaction to the sudden stock-out situation caused by a clearance sale. There are certain strategies for disposing of excess inventory without causing the bullwhip effect. This is one area where the sales and marketing function can have an adverse impact on the realization of ROI from SCM systems.

Advances in technology and globalization find firms faced with shorter product cycle times and increasing pressure to be customer-focused. Increasingly, IT is being called upon to provide the competitive agility and flexibility to meet these challenges. The classic pull solutions that we reviewed in this chapter are one end of the spectrum. Pure network economy solutions lie at the other end. Market economy solutions are based on forecasting; thus they push products to customers based on expert opinion or historical data. In contrast, network economy solutions emphasize responsiveness to customer needs and are designed to enable the customer to pull product through the supply chain. Network economy solutions are the focus of the next chapter.

CHAPTER 5

Network Economy Solutions

When we showed the supply chain relationships and technologies for the market economy in the previous chapter, we illustrated one extreme of the trade-off between production efficiency and customer responsiveness. Supply chain solutions for the market economy focus on production efficiency, based on demand forecasting. In contrast, the network economy solution has the customer at its center, pulling products and services as needed from the supply chain.

For ease of exposition, we will refer to the network economy model as the *pull model*. In the pull model, the entire supply chain is engaged in satisfying the customer's product, service, and support needs on an ongoing basis. In traditional supply chains supporting the push model, usually only the downstream partners and the channel master interact directly with the customer. In contrast, for the pull model, most trading partners of the supply chain will be required to interact directly with the customer. Unlike the hierarchical relationships illustrated in the previous chapter, in the pull model there is a no linear flow of goods, services, and information to and from the customer. Rather, the trading partners collaborate among themselves and communicate with the customer to provide customized products and services at the customer's point of need (refer to Figure 1.1). To highlight this difference, we will refer to the supply chain supporting the pull model as a *supply web*. The supply web is organized for communication and collaboration across all its trading partners with the goal of full responsiveness to customer needs.

The Pull Model

Figure 5.1 shows the customer-centered pull model and the supporting supply web. The customer can configure and order products and services through a variety of options—for example, physical outlets, phone, fax, email, or Web forms.

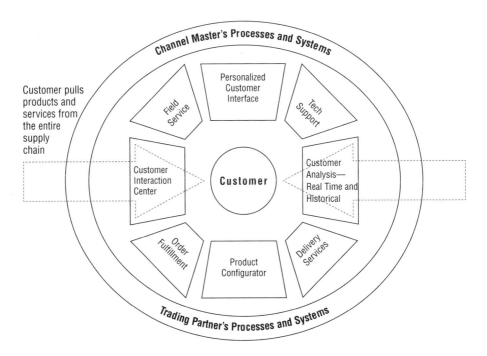

Customer pulls products and services from the entire supply chain

Figure 5.1: The supply web's processes and systems surround the customer.

The customer can configure the product to the exact specifications that meet his or her requirements. On submitting an order, the customer receives immediate feedback on the date the product will be shipped and other pertinent information, such as delivery firm information, for example. The customer is also provided with tools to check the status of the order through a variety of options, ranging from traditional (service centers) to technology-based self-service (telephone, Internet-based inquiry capabilities, etc.) The status notifications throughout the order fulfillment process can be customized to suit the customer requirements. The customer could also opt to receive automatic notification from the supply web when the product is shipped, via email, a phone message, fax, or regular mail.

In the ideal pull model, every shipped product is built to order per customer specifications. The order fulfillment process is visible to all trading partners involved in sourcing, making, and delivering the end product to the customer. Trading partners—from upstream raw materials and component suppliers to contract manufacturers, warehousing, and shipping services—interact directly with this fulfillment process. All trading partners collaborate to provide a single face to the customer. The customer is oblivious to the fact that multiple firms are handling various elements of building, shipping, and providing postsales service and support for the product. Business networks—internal to the firm and across the supply web—would utilize Internet technologies to present a single face to the customer.

Reach and Range

Reach and range are critical concepts in the context of selecting various supply chain or Web technologies. These simple yet powerful concepts can help managers evaluate supply chain integration technologies along business functionalities without getting overwhelmed by technology minutiae. Peter G. W. Keen introduced these terms in the early 1990s, and, despite the ever-changing technology integration landscape, they have remained relevant.

The concept of *reach* as it relates to IT infrastructure refers to the capability of technology to allow interaction with other systems within the firm and across the trading partner network. Specific technology families can be mapped to different levels of reach. On one end of the reach spectrum for a technology are stand-alone systems within the business unit. An example of such a stand-alone dedicated system would be a mainframe-based inventory system accessible via dedicated terminals only in the warehouse. Moving along the spectrum, reach expands to interaction with business units across multiple geographic locations within the firm. At the other end of the spectrum reach includes the ability to interact with all units within the firm and all customers and suppliers, irrespective of the underlying technologies. Simple examples of technologies with such broad reach are phone, fax, or PC-based Web browsers. Figure 5.2 illustrates the reach and range spectrums.

The *range* of an integration technology describes the nature of the interaction the technology facilitates. The range of a technology at one end of the spectrum starts with the ability to send simple messages. A simple mes-

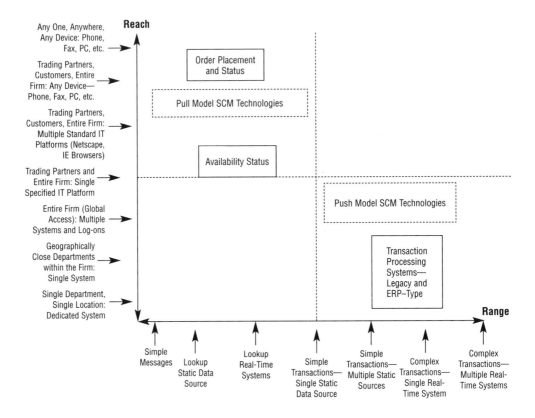

Figure 5.2: Reach and range of SCM functionality. Adapted from Peter G. W. Keen,
***Shaping the Future*, Harvard Business School Press, Boston, 1991.**

sage could be an email, fax, or a database query. Depending on the reach of
the technology, these messages can be accessed within the business unit,
within the firm, or across the supply web. Range progresses along the spectrum to offer query information of varying complexity from simple look-
ups to complex queries of real-time systems. The extreme end of the range
spectrum provides the ability to perform complex transactions across multiple applications in real-time. For example, a complex transaction may
involve checking the availability of product from an inventory system,
scheduling its delivery through the shipping system, and getting credit
authorization from the credit bureau while creating the billing information.

The different technology families shown along the reach spectrum in
Figure 5.2 vary in their ability to provide range. The technology family at

the single department, single location is typified by mainframe or minicomputer systems dedicated to a single task—such as receiving or accounts payable functions. They support an integrated set of functions that span the range spectrum from allowing simple messages within the department up to complex real-time transactions within a single location. They do not have the ability to perform transactions across multiple systems. The next families of technologies in the reach spectrum are typified by client/server technologies that allow departments within the firm and across the firm to access multiple back-end mainframe systems and perform complex transactions spanning multiple real-time systems. The next family of technologies allows the trading partners and all departments across the firm to access multiple transaction systems. These technologies fall in the intranet and extranet categories. The point to note here is that as we move up the reach spectrum, the ability to perform complex real-time transactions decreases due to the number of systems that have to be synchronized for real-time transaction processing. Ultimately, the technology families at the extreme of the reach spectrum, such as phone or fax, have restricted range to perform simple actions such as passing messages, looking up static data sources, and performing simple transactions with a single system.

Correspondingly, simple messages have a broad reach across all technology families, whereas complex transactions across multiple real-time systems can only have limited reach within a single location or firm. It is important to understand this trade-off when making choices about whether to integrate processes with simple messages or data queries as opposed to complex real-time transactions.

In Figure 5.2, the functionality needed to surround the customer is mapped onto the reach and range characteristics. For example, the position of the order status module in the figure shows that it needs access to multiple systems within the firm and across the supply web. While it does not support simple or complex transactions, it allows lookup from operational data stores and sends that information back to the customer. Similarly, ascertaining the availability of raw materials and components to promise a shipping date requires the ability to look up availability status data. This functionality is also illustrated on the reach and range map.

It is important for managers to understand these concepts and use them to evaluate various integration and infrastructure technologies needed to support the pull model solution. During the technology selection process (discussed in greater detail in Chapter 8), we will show how to map the reach and range characteristics of all SCM functionalities by product or service need. This map, in conjunction with the strategic goals of the firm, can then be used to narrow the technology options that the firm seeks to evaluate.

Customization and the Supply Chain

Many firms have corporate mission statements that include the promise "to develop and distribute customized products." If the incremental cost of producing an additional unit of customized product is negligible, the firm can offer mass customization. This mass customization is possible for certain product categories (digitized products and services) where the marginal cost of production for a customized product is negligible. There is a limit on the amount of customization that a product with physical properties which require storage, handling, and conventional delivery can have. This limit on customization of physical products is dictated by the ability of the firm to produce and sell the product at a price attractive to potential customers. We will discuss specific product categories and the supporting supply chains within the context of customization.

Digitized Products

Information technologies with the appropriate level of reach and range are deployed to support the customer-centered vision depicted in Figure 5.1. The products and services that can be pulled to the customer's unique requirements depend largely on their physical attributes and the value-add process. Information services (such as financial services) and digitized products (such as music or electronic books) can be customized in potentially unlimited combinations to suit individual needs. For example, certain music distributors allow consumers to customize a compact disc (CD) containing songs of their choice from multiple artists. This unique selection is produced with customizable artwork on the CD and shipped to the customer's location.

At the heart of a decision to purchase a customized CD is the consumer's desire to be able to listen to music tracks of choice anytime and anywhere. At present, however, the use of the CD medium limits the consumer's ability to play the music, because a CD player is required. In the near future, given the digitized content of the music, it will be possible to sell to the consumer rights to listen to the music at will—irrespective of the medium. The consumer paying for the music will be allowed through some form of authentication to listen to the customized tracks using a radio, a computer, or any other audio device with the capability of receiving the music data stream.

Another product with potentially unlimited customization possibilities is the electronic book. Certain electronic book vendors today allow their customers to download selected books and magazines to a digital book reader. The customer pays the license fees for the books, magazines, and journals and downloads and accesses the materials as needed. This liberates digitizable content from the limitations of the physical world. In the very near future, it is likely that consumers will be able to take both their music collections and extensive library to the beach by carrying an audio device and electronic book reader with wireless reception capability. For digital products, the supply chains that support the old physical model are considerably different than those for the pull model. As the physical process of printing CDs and books is eliminated, costs are reduced considerably. Supply chain costs relating to coordinating the printing presses and acquiring raw materials to produce the products are significantly reduced.

Physical Products

Customization and building to order become increasingly problematic as we move from digital to physical products. Dell Corporation is often cited as an example of a firm that has a pull supply chain. The customers themselves configure the PCs they plan to buy, specifying customizable accessories. The PCs are then built to order and shipped within a few days to the customers.

What does this practice imply for Dell's supply chain? Any order placed at a Dell Web site is immediately shared with Dell's suppliers. Based on the immediate feedback from the suppliers, Dell is able to provide notification of the expected date of shipment within a short period of time. Dell prides itself that it measures its inventory levels in hours rather than days.[1] This means that the suppliers to Dell have to acquire and store some of the mate-

---

[1] Joan Magretta, "The Power of Virtual Integration: An Interview with Dell Computer's Michael Dell," *Harvard Business Review,* Mar.–Apr. 1998, pp. 73–84.

rials and components needed for Dell's orders. The limitations imposed by the physical world on making and shipping PC components dictate a lead time to acquire these components. This lead time requires Dell's suppliers to use projected demand to acquire raw materials to support Dell's customers. Dell and its suppliers use detailed forecasts to project demand for various combinations of Dell's computers. These forecasts form the basis for its suppliers to store and supply components to meet actual demand. Dell also helps its suppliers dispose of components that could not be used due to product phase-out or incorrect demand forecast. Clearly, in the world of physical goods, very close collaboration between the channel master and suppliers is needed if the pull model is to be used, particularly if the channel master's product lines face intense price competition.

Limitations Imposed by Property, Plant, and Equipment

Now let's consider a different type of product and a different type of firm. With Dell, production facilities are idled when there are no customer orders to build to. However, Dell's investments in PPE are significantly lower than the investments of an automobile manufacturer, for example. An automobile manufacturer can't allow production lines to be driven by actual customer orders. The investments in PPE are enormous, and production lines need to be working at a given capacity utilization to realize benefits. However, some car manufacturers are developing the capacity to build and deliver a car to customer specifications within a few days. These manufacturers will be using both the push model and the pull model: They will be making cars both to actual order and to forecasted demand to maximize the utilization of PPE.

Given the large investments in PPE across the automotive supply chain, one way to modify operations to shift to a customer-centered pull model is to "reinvent" the production process. The "reinvented process" (based on Hewlett-Packard's model) postpones the incorporation of customizable features such as color, interior fabric, accessories, and instrumentation to just prior to shipment to dealers or customers.[2] Despite this "reinvention," however, cars may be manufactured without final customization due to a mis-

---

[2] E. Feitzinger and H. L. Lee, "Mass Customization at Hewlett-Packard: The Power of Postponement," *Harvard Business Review*, Jan.–Feb. 1997.

match between overall projected demand and actual customized orders. As multiple tiers of suppliers are involved, each having to ensure optimum capacity utilization, moving to a pure pull model (built to order without any demand forecasts) would create time delays due to component bottlenecks and would make the price of a car very high.

The manufacturing constraints illustrated here have certainly not escaped the attention of executives in the automobile industry. In fact, there is a great deal of debate in many manufacturing firms about what products they are actually selling and where their competitive advantage is derived from. Legend has it that in the early 1990s, at an annual meeting of automotive executives from various companies, the chairman of Toyota remarked how the laws of physics are driving the aerodynamic design of cars to the most optimal shape. As a consequence, he found he could hardly tell the difference between Toyota cars and those of his competitors without getting close enough to read the company nameplates. In addition, over the past few years, there has been increasing trend toward leasing cars as opposed to outright ownership. Both of these factors have influenced a trend toward a shift in car manufacturers' focus from manufacturing to selling the automotive "experience" to customers.

Traditionally, the customer does not interact with the car manufacturer after buying a car. With leasing, the car manufacturer is increasingly in touch with the consumer, allowing the manufacturer to provide additional services related to automotive use, such as new accessories or information. In essence, the car manufacturer is recasting itself as a provider of the entire automotive "experience": reliable transportation, services helping consumers to reach their destination, services to make the trip more enjoyable (online entertainment for the children), advice on suitable destinations, and recommendations on other products and services that will enhance the experience. Hence, the focus of the car manufacturer shifts from production to sensing and responding to consumers' automotive experience needs—be they basic transportation or transportation-related products and services.

To implement this new role, firms have been shifting more manufacturing responsibility to their suppliers. For example, Fiat in Italy and VW in Brazil have production facilities where the suppliers run the assembly line. Innovative steps like this can allow even a firm in the traditional manufacturing industries to be customer-centered.

Benefits of the Pull Model

Recall that Figure 4.1 listed the visible and invisible costs in a firm. To reduce the biggest chunk of invisible costs requires collaborative processes within the firm and with the members of the supply web. The benefits accrue from intermediation between the trading partners across the supply web. By contrast, disintermediation of bureaucratic overhead within the procurement process reduces the visible transaction related costs. Using IT to implement a pull model approach to providing goods and services has both coordination and transaction cost benefits.

Allowing customers to configure and order products of their choice online has considerable impact on customer satisfaction and customer retention. More importantly, taking an order via automated entry reduces the cost per order significantly as compared to taking orders through conventional means. There is less risk of transcription errors because the customer enters the order once and the automatically generated, correct order is passed directly to the firm's supply web for sourcing, manufacture, and delivery. According to survey research conducted at the University of Texas, 69 percent of firms reported an increase in revenue as a result of allowing customer access to IT systems for configuring orders or researching information online.[3]

On the supplier end, there is no time lapse or filtered or transcribed view of the customer requirements. This puts the onus on the suppliers to ensure the customer's needs are met. As we will illustrate in the next section, this is the biggest organizational and cultural hurdle to overcome. The customer becomes a customer to every trading partner in the supply web. This idea sounds very appealing, but it is difficult to implement. Consider that in most firms access to customers is typically claimed by sales and marketing. If these departments zealously guard access to customers from other departments *within* their own firms, how likely are they to permit the supply chain to have direct customer contact?

In Chapter 4, we used the musical analogy of a symphony to describe market economy or push model supply chain solutions. The network economy or pull model supply chain solutions can be likened to a jazz score. During the performance of a jazz ensemble, every player can innovate and improvise within certain parameters of the score. Similarly, the supply web

---

[3] Anitesh Barua et al., "Making E-Business Pay: Eight Key Drivers for Operational Success," *IT Pro,* IEEE, Nov.–Dec. 2000.

in a pull model strives to satisfy customer needs while working within quality and delivery objective parameters. How exactly the trading partners serve customer needs is left to the individual suppliers, who collaborate within the supply web to ensure that customer needs are met. Allowing the supply web to directly support the product and service delivery needs of the customer frees the channel master to focus on sensing changing customer needs and keeping up with product and service innovations.

Additional profitable revenue can be generated by cross-selling and up-selling to customers at multiple touch points in the supply web, such as customer care or field service centers. Such added opportunities can more easily be generated, because the channel master can focus on analyzing customer needs rather than production efficiency. The benefits from increased customer retention rates and revenue from repeat customers through cross-selling and up-selling make a significant dent in the invisible costs in the selling and general administrative expense category.

Not only does the pull model reduce invisible costs and enhance customer satisfaction, it also enables the company to be a more frequent innovator to make a product or service more compelling. This ability will ensure that a firm's product rarely goes through the typical product life cycle in which a product eventually becomes like a commodity. For example, GEICO changed the commodity nature of car insurance by servicing the customer need for transportation after an accident. When a GEICO customer reports a car accident to the insurance company, an automatic alert is placed with the nearest car rental agency ordering a car to the driver's location.[4] Adding features or auxiliary services sets the product apart from the offerings of competitors, thus reducing price competition, enhancing revenue and margins, and improving customer retention.

Intermediation based on collaborative infrastructure necessary for supporting the pull model is the biggest source of potential benefits. Let's revisit our iceberg analogy. We illustrated how the pooling of common direct and indirect raw materials procurement for the entire supply web yields savings in the invisible component of the iceberg (refer to Figure 4.1). In addition, outsourcing MRO purchases to an integrated MRO supplier with specific financial targets provides benefits through reduction of administrative overhead for all firms within the supply web. The internal procurement functions across the trading partners can then focus exclusively on developing

---

[4] Heather Harreld, "Pick-Up Artists," *CIO Magazine,* Nov. 1, 2000.

and executing critical direct raw materials and component strategies, such as advance commitment to purchase, thus reducing landed costs for the entire supply web.

Finally, the collaborative infrastructure reduces product development and introduction cycle times. As the entire supply web is jointly working on new product development in a lockstep fashion, actual production can begin shortly after design freeze due to the concurrent nature of the product design and manufacturing process. Furthermore, competitive flexibility and agility are increased as a result of the infrastructure's capability for introducing rapid and frequent product and service enhancements. Given that there are no tight integration requirements in the pull model, new supply web partners can be brought in as needed for producing and servicing new product offerings. As illustrated in Figure 5.2, the reach and range of pull model technology infrastructure tends to be in the top left quadrant.

These benefits are examples of significant revenue enhancements, profit improvements, and cost reductions in a variety of selling and general administrative categories that are not as readily apparent as those associated with transaction processing. However, they will only accrue to those firms that make the necessary organizational, cultural, and process changes to foster a collaborative mind-set geared toward serving a common customer. The pull model's technology component is a small factor in realizing the benefits from customer-focused supply webs.

The organizational and process alignment needed to successfully deploy and realize the benefits from the pull model's technology solutions are discussed in greater detail in Chapter 6. A firm organized along traditional functional lines, a common practice to support the push model, cannot transform overnight into pull model firm. Fortunately, this is usually not an either-or question. There are many stages of collaboration that a firm can engage in. In many instances it may not be necessary for a firm to completely move to a pull model. Depending on the product, its competitive positioning, and the supporting supply chain, a firm may find that a lower-level collaborative stage meets all of the firm's strategic business goals. Consider the often-mentioned example of the Wal-Mart data warehouse. Wal-Mart's suppliers have access to information about how their products are doing in each store, allowing them to proactively manage their manufacturing and distribution activities to match actual forecasted events in the stores.

Stages of Collaboration

The shift to collaborative, customer-focused processes and supporting technologies can be viewed as taking place in four distinct stages, each of which has its benefits and risks. These are shown in Figure 5.3. The least complex way to realign the processes of the firm and its supply web to focus on customer needs starts with a basic exchange of information about a customer. From an IT technology standpoint, this functionality can be placed in the top left quadrant of Figure 5.2. The figure shows an associated process and technology infrastructure that allows suppliers and customers to communicate with one another across the supply web irrespective of disparate supporting technologies.

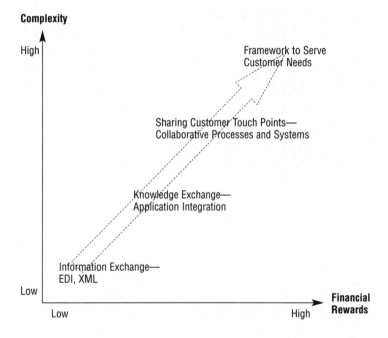

Figure 5.3: The shift to a collaborative, customer-focused model and associated rewards.

Information Exchange

The information exchange stage does not follow a sequential path, such as the one shown in Figure 4.2. Rather, messages relating to customer needs flow across the supply web in all directions to support the customer's product and service requirements (refer to Figure 1.1). This type of information flow can be supported easily with technologies such as EDI and Internet-based communication platforms. Implementing the processes and supporting technologies for this stage is not very complex. However, the impact on revenue enhancement, profit improvement, and cost reductions are correspondingly low.

Knowledge Exchange

The next stage of collaboration involves knowledge exchange about the customer among the trading partners. This requires more than the sharing of basic information.

For example, an athletic footwear manufacturer finds that in response to the winning record of a professional basketball team, the demand for a particular type of basketball shoe in this team's region has increased. The athletic footwear maker can then share this knowledge with its Asian suppliers and its customers, the retail chains. The suppliers will respond by quickly making and shipping more shoes of this particular type. The retailers can potentially shift stock that is already on warehouse shelves in other regions and ship it to the location where it is needed. Because fashion tastes are fickle, a quick response by the entire supply chain is necessary to take advantage of this market opportunity. This form of knowledge exchange is depicted on the reach and range map (see Figure 5.2) as having the functionality to query in-store inventory systems at retail outlets. On the reach axis this functionality requires that the firm interface with suppliers and customers with a similar IT base. On the range axis, such functionality allows firms to query operational data stores. For example, the athletic footwear company in our example would be able to get a real-time picture of the retail outlets' sales by shoe style and initiate a proactive response to ensure ready availability.

Sharing Customer Touch Points

The third stage of collaboration requires the actual sharing of customer touch points within the firm and across the entire supply web. Decisions to service customer needs are taken as necessary by any member of the supply web. Consider the example of a car that is brought in for maintenance and excessive instances of a component failure are detected for that particular make and model—say a spark plug. Without waiting for approval from the channel master, on receipt of notifications from the service shops, the spark plug manufacturer specifies a different type and quality of spark plug to reduce the failure rates. The channel master and other trading partners are also notified of this component change. Component shipments to the manufacturing line are changed to reflect the higher quality of spark plugs.

Similarly, if the service department of an automobile dealership notices that adding a particular accessory would improve the customer experience with a particular product feature, it would try to cross-sell or up-sell that component during the service process. Given the problems associated with overcoming organizational boundaries and internal politics within a firm, this relationship needs to be well structured and accompanied by proper incentives. The financial returns from this approach are substantial, but the technologies needed to support this type of activity are more complex.

Figure 5.2 shows that the reach and range of technologies within the firm are located in the lower right-hand quadrant. Within the firm, multiple departments must be allowed access to perform simple to moderately complex transactions across multiple applications. Continuing the previous example, the service bay technical manager at the dealership may need access to the sales catalog and order entry application for cross-selling. In addition, members of the supply web may need technology that maps into the upper left-hand quadrant. This will allow the suppliers to perform simple transactions across all systems within the firm, even those with dissimilar technology bases.

Framework to Serve Customer Needs across the Supply Web

The fourth and final stage of collaborative effort requires the channel master to focus exclusively on sensing and responding to customer needs, thereby providing the framework for the other members of the supply web to serve the customer. The integration technology needed to enable such intense collaboration falls squarely in the top right-hand corner of Figure 5.2: Customers and suppliers will be able to access multiple systems to perform simple to moderately complex transactions across the entire supply web.

What is unique to stage four is that the supply web is not static. The channel master brings suppliers into the web as dictated by customer needs. Similarly, if customers no longer desire a product or the channel master can't sell that product profitably, suppliers associated with that product are removed from the collaborative infrastructure.

A good nontechnical example illustrating a stage-four collaborative framework comes from the grocery industry. In certain affluent neighborhoods, traditional grocery stores have recast themselves as marketplaces to serve premium foods and beverages to their clientele. The marketplace provides the floor space and administrative infrastructure for the baker, meat, poultry, fruit, and other specialty vendors. Individual vendors take care of their own customers, allowing the marketplace owner to focus on analyzing aggregate scanner data to ensure that the overall product or service needs of customers are met. This allows the specialty grocers to focus exclusively on the customer needs in their specialty segment because they don't have to divert their attention to activities related to maintaining the physical plant of the store. The entire strategy is focused on understanding customer needs and delivering high-quality produce with value-added services (such as an in-store butcher) that customers want. In return for quality and service, customers are willing to pay higher prices, thus providing higher margins in a fairly low-margin industry. In this marketplace—speciality store—example, close collaboration is mostly achieved by co-locating the different businesses. Extrapolating this model to other services and manufactured goods involves a tremendous amount of complexity because maintaining such a rich collaboration requires installing and maintaining highly complex integration and infrastructure technologies.

Technology as the Disruptor

During the fourth stage of collaboration, technology acts as a constant disruptor of the value chain. Allowing collaboration with firms that do not have similar technologies to those of the channel master or the existing supply web requires constant tearing down and rebuilding of the supply chain or the supply web. If a trading partner is not capable of adequately serving customer needs, another trading partner who can is immediately brought in.

Processes and organizational relationships inside and outside the firms constantly change as customer needs evolve. This disruptive property of technology is very different from the process-enabling role of technology in the push model discussed in the previous chapter, where the emphasis was on operational optimization. In the pull model, the channel master is constantly forced to destroy and rebuild the supply web to procure goods and services that the customer values because the focus is on improved margins from innovation and customer service. As a result, the channel master has to perform continuous cost-benefit analyses to determine the value of serving the customer with a particular product or service.

Service Chain

The concept of service chains was introduced in the previous chapter. Service chains are based on process mapping and alignment across the trading partner firms to enable collaboration in the service production and delivery process. Let us look at an example from the service industry to illustrate the process mapping, alignment, and collaboration needed for effective service chain deployments. Las Vegas's Bellagio hotel screened 84,000 candidates, interviewed 27,000 of them, and hired 9600 people within a period of 24 weeks.[5] Changing and replacing the old hiring procedures and implementing a new process and supporting information systems accomplished this feat. All prospective employees were treated like blue-chip customers. The employee/customer was the focal point of all processes in the system design. The employee interaction system was redesigned multiple times based on employee feedback to make it as easy to use as an ATM. To achieve the seemingly impossible goals required a fundamental redesign of processes to focus on the customer. All groups needed to collaborate to make this process successful. After the hiring objectives were met, the technology to support the system was prepared for deployment at other customer-focused services.

Elements of a Solution to Support the Pull Model

We saw in the previous chapter that the focus of SCM systems in the push model is the operational optimization of physical assets of the firm. By contrast, the pull model SCM systems are geared toward financial optimization of the knowledge assets relating to customer needs. Revenue and profit are generated from outstanding customer service and frequent innovation.

Recall that market economy push solutions incorporate best practices for SCM functionality, such as forecasting aggregate demand for a product,

---

[5] Bill Breen, "Full House," *Fast Company*, No. 42, Jan. 2001.

translating the demand plan to tactical sourcing and distribution plans, and finally translating the optimum plan to production schedules. These types of functionality are embedded in software offerings from technology vendors, for example, I-2, SAP, and Manugistics.

Some technology vendors claim that their products support both push models and pull models. They do provide added functionality for supplier collaboration in planning, forecasting, inventory replenishment, and similar areas. However, the core engine of all software packages supporting the push model is based on synchronizing the sourcing, production, and delivery activities within the firm and across the supply chain. Best practices for optimal use of assets (through scheduling) and reduced freight (planned logistics) are embedded in these systems. Deriving the full benefits from these best practices depends largely on production to forecasted demand, the basic premise of the push model.

The pull model, in contrast, requires best practices for sensing and responding to customer needs within the firm and across the supply chain. The number of different customer touch points throughout the supply web means that there is a multitude of different approaches to sensing and responding to customer needs, and thus no single set of best practices is available. Therefore, best practices for sensing and responding to customer needs cannot be embedded in application software. However, the push and the pull models can and will coexist within the same supply chain/web. For example, while a firm may be buying commodity inputs and *customizing* them in their value-added process (using the pull model), it is most likely that upstream commodity manufacturers are using a push model for their operations.

Aggregating Customer Touch Points in the Pull Model

The fundamental capability that a pull solution provides is the ability to combine all customer touch points within the supply web and present a single face to the customer. Customers should not realize that they are dealing with multiple firms, let alone be aware of the distinction between sales and service within the firm. Figure 5.4 illustrates this concept.

The customer is able to interact with the channel master using a variety of access methods, such as a telephone or the Internet. At the interaction point (the interaction "front end"), the channel master, trading partner, and

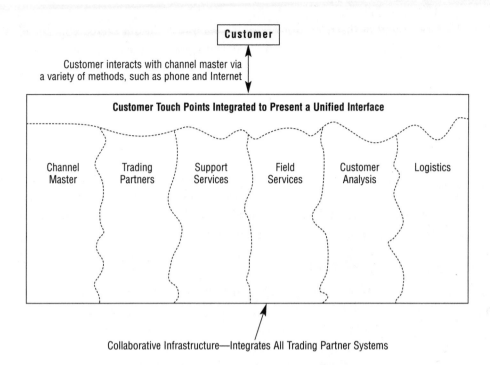

Figure 5.4: Pull model collaborative structure.

other customer touch points are seamlessly integrated, allowing the customer to pull customized products and services from the supply web. The zigzag dotted lines between various trading partners highlight that collaboration and coordination among trading partners occur as needed for a particular product or service and that the organizational boundaries are fuzzy, or, to use a biological metaphor, even permeable. Process-oriented best practices do not enhance the customer responsiveness of a supply web; in contrast, following best practices for sensing and responding to customer needs requires the members of the supply web to provide the necessary infrastructure to communicate, collaborate, and coordinate their activities.

The customer-focused technology platform should provide functionality that acquires customers, retains them, and enhances their experience. Currently, this set of functionalities is offered through software vendors of customer relationship management (CRM) systems. To support the pull model, CRM systems provide integration points to different functional areas within the firm and across the supply web. On the customer end, the technology solution must offer the following four features, at a minimum:

- Personalized interaction
- Self-service
- Product and service configuration
- Customer analysis

The primary purpose of these technology features in conjunction with aligned processes and alliance relationships between the partners in the supply web is to make the customers feel that every touch point has all the knowledge required to serve their needs.

Personalized Interaction

Personalization features enable customers to configure the look and feel of their interaction with the firm. Examples of such individualization are personalized Web pages, email alerts on specific events (such as order shipment, sale notifications), and phone alerts. Contrary to a widespread misconception, personalization does not *require* a customizable Web page. The Internet is just one channel a customer may choose to interact with the firm. The features of the customer interface that were previously listed should be provided through as many interaction channels as possible—be they Web-based, phone, fax, or regular U.S. mail. A standard catalog does not satisfy the requirements for personalized interaction; the experience of the customer has to be tailored to his or her individual requirements. Although some paper catalogs for high-end products and services are highly customized in content, based on each customer's past buying habits and expressed interests, this form of customization is a lot easier to achieve in the online world.

A combination of electronic and manual processes, offered through a variety of channels, yields the personalized functionality that a customer is likely to want and use. For example, one customer may choose to receive a notification on his or her Web site when the order is shipped. A different customer may choose to receive a phone call or postcard regarding the shipment. The information is the same—the channel of interaction is different. The customer can explicitly select his or her personalized interaction or the systems can proactively change the interaction based on past behavior.

For a typical mature firm, personalization is very difficult to provide. Usually, information about the customer is scattered among multiple systems of record. Combining and analyzing the customer information from many disparate sources within the organization has been a challenge for the average firm. This situation is not likely to improve. Especially with the advent of Web-based interfaces, enormous amounts of data about customers are being collected. When customers access a Web site, all interaction activities—ranging from which site a customer came from to the order in which the customer clicked through various screen options to the point at which the customer exited the Web page—are recorded. This data is called the click stream, and mountains of click-stream data are generated when customers navigate through a Web site.

Analyzing all customer-related data and presenting a uniform knowledgeable face is the biggest challenge of personalization. In addition, customer information will be scattered across the supply web. When a channel master selects a personalization technology, the firm should ensure that customer data across the supply web is stored accessibly and becomes the property of the firm. All information that helps develop knowledge about the customer is to be treated on a par with the physical assets of the push model. Portal technologies are currently available to help firms present a single face to the customer. These technologies will be discussed in more detail in Chapter 7.

Self-Service

Self-service capability is another major feature of a pull solution. Customers want the ability to place an order, inquire about a product or service, and receive support 24 hours a day and 7 days a week (24x7). Irrespective of the channel being used, self-service features are necessary for customer satisfaction. How do firms deal with this requirement? Certain financial services firms have deployed customer service centers around the globe that provide 24-hour support. Support calls are passed from one time zone to the next along with the setting sun.

From the suppliers' standpoint, customer orders can and should be transmitted immediately to the supply web. The self-service feature may require a direct interface to the supplier systems to provide information such as availability of components and accessories, shipping date, and package tracking information. Thus the members of the supply web must allow access to their internal systems. However, the supply web's responsibility goes beyond providing access. They will all have to ensure the same level of availability from their systems to support 24x7 capability. Minimizing the number of supply web systems being accessed to serve a customer can provide increased access reliability.

All members of the supply web should provide a common customer service center to consolidate multiple customer interaction points. The self-service functionality must be designed to hide the fact that multiple firms may be collaborating to support the customer. A loosely coupled architecture facilitates this type of interaction and mitigates the risk from system downtime across the supply web (discussed in greater detail in Chapter 7). When defining supporting processes and selecting technologies, a reliable, accurate self-service function is a critical success factor.

Product and Service Configuration

Product configuration capability is related to self-service, but is a distinct functionality that has tremendous implications for the supply chain. A customer may choose to configure products via interaction at a Web site or by giving their preferences to a customer service representative over the phone. Many PC manufacturers allow customers to configure the systems to their exact specifications. The customer also has the option of choosing from an array of configurable options and price the overall system without having to complete the order.

Note that additional information can be gathered by analyzing the decisions of the customer, even if the customer does not complete the purchase. For example, the firm may learn that a customer has displayed an interest for an audio component, but, on pricing the overall system, the customer seems reluctant to place the order. If the system can locate a PC package that provides the audio component desired by the customer at a lower price, it should proactively suggest the alternative, either automatically on the Web site or through a customer service representative on the phone.

Using personalization data gathered explicitly or through click-stream analysis, firms accumulate knowledge about customer preferences for a particular product. This knowledge can be used to guide the customer through product configuration options that the customer cares about. For example, if it is known that a customer selecting options for purchasing a car has children, a built-in child seat option should be at the top of the list.

Once a customer is satisfied with the configured product and places the order, the order information must be released immediately to the members of the supply web for fulfillment. Customers will also want to know when the product can be delivered. Close collaboration between all members of the supply web is required here to provided an accurate estimate of the scheduled delivery date to the customer. All involved members of the supply web must provide accurate information on available components and lead-time information.

Customer Analysis

The last piece of functionality in the customer-focused technology platform is real-time and historical customer analysis. Real-time customer analysis monitors the customer's interaction with the firm during online or phone interactions. If the customer seems to be having difficulty or is stalled at a particular point, for example during order placement, product configuration, or locating technical FAQs, the analytical engine detects and recommends proactive measures to service the customer.

Similarly, historical analysis of customer inquiries that did not result in an order may indicate a necessity to change the price, the features, or the order placement process to improve the chances of closing the sale. Historical analysis generates knowledge about the customer from past transactions and from his or her interaction with areas such as customer service, the return merchandise authorization department, and the warranty department. This knowledge can be used to drive the personalization capabilities and improve customer retention rates and enhancement opportunities.

All members of the supply web have to allow access to data about customer interaction freely and as needed to all other trading partners. This is critical because, for example, supplier A may need information from the warranty database of supplier B to address issues relating to customer satisfaction with A's core product. Instead of being wary that this type of information could be misused to assign blame, it should be shared without any reservations with the goal of better understanding and supporting the customer. It is up to the channel master and the supporting supply web to leverage knowledge about the customer by offering goods and services tailored to meet and exceed customer expectations.

The system features supporting the pull model are clearly interrelated. Although each feature can be implemented on its own, truly "surrounding and serving the customer" requires implementing all four features. In Figure 5.2 the technology infrastructure needed for the pull model is depicted in the top left-hand quadrant, whereas the push model is in the bottom right-hand quadrant. Managers, but especially information systems staff, must understand that it is the organizational and process barriers more than the technology that can make a customer-centered model difficult to implement across the supply web. All trading partners need to collaborate behind the scenes of the customer interaction to fully serve the customer. A new category of software called partner relationship management systems is emerging that seeks to provide this type of collaborative functionality with customer interaction points.

Toward a Supply Chain Community

A supply chain/web that provides the functionality of the pull model is a first step toward becoming a supply chain community. A *supply chain community* is a group of firms each specializing in a particular area, such as contract manufacturing, order fulfillment, logistics services, etc., which collaborate to satisfy an emerging customer need. The trading partners within the community share the costs and profits in an equitable manner. The focus is on collaboration to meet customers' needs without the barrier of arm's-length transactions between the key trading partners. Instead, the firms in the supply chain community pursue long-term-alliance relationships, based on mutual trust.

Obviously a supply chain community must consist of trading partners who offer a unique value in terms of serving customer needs. A commodity component supplier with multiple substitutes that is not a critical input for the finished product cannot be a member of the supply chain community. The membership of a firm is determined by the unique added value that the firm brings to the community in servicing the needs of the customer.

The leadership role in organizing a supply chain community can initially be taken by any one of the trading partners who identifies an unmet product or service niche. This is in obvious contrast to the push model of providing goods and services, where new products and services are developed and brought to market with most of the sales, marketing, product development, and delivery functions captive to the firm. The supply chain community coalesces around an unmet opportunity to bring new products and services to market, and it disperses when it is no longer profitable to do so.

This form of organization would not have been possible without the infrastructure provided by Internet technologies. Does this mean that the old functional form of an organization is irrelevant? Absolutely not! To be a low-cost producer, a firm has to be organized along functional lines. Even in a supply chain community, there must be members that have efficient manufacturing capabilities. The need to balance efficiency with flexibility is discussed in greater detail in Chapter 6. However, as an organizational form, the supply chain community provides greater flexibility in discovering and serving new product and service niches.

The main benefit of organizing in a supply community accrues from specialization benefits. Greater specialization results in greater depth of knowledge. Greater depth of knowledge, in turn, results in greater ability to innovate. Specialization allows firms to develop their expertise by deploying processes and technologies focused exclusively within their narrow field of expertise. The supply chain community invites members to join who have the specialization necessary to develop an emerging product or service need. Thus supply communities are most appropriate for products and services that are innovative. It is during the innovation and early growth stages that products and services garner the highest margins. As the novelty of a product wears off and it acquires commodity status, the supply chain community may disband, allowing more efficient producers to service this commoditized market.

Competitive Agility

Implementing a pull solution allows a firm tremendous competitive agility. The underlying infrastructure (organization, processes, and technology) is focused on loose collaboration and not the tight process and technology integration required for a push solution—within the firm and across the supply chain. It is quite probable that a firm following the pull model will outsource most or all of its non-customer-related functions, primarily so that the firm's innovative capabilities will not be hindered by investments in PPE geared toward manufacturing a specific product. Firms are reluctant to introduce new products if the equipment they have invested in is specific to the production of their existing products. New products might cannibalize old ones and render the specific investments in PPE obsolete.

Tightly coupled information systems, internal to the firm as well as those that support the coordination with specific supply chain partners, also represent specific investments. Similar to machines, they may be rendered obsolete if the product or service offering of a firm changes drastically. However, newer Web technologies using a loosely coupled architecture are more flexible and cause less locking in to a particular technology solution.

Due to the loosely coupled architecture of the supply web, trading partners can be brought in as needed to respond to a competitor's move. However, most firms do not have the luxury to start from scratch. Thus the implementation of the pull solution will have to occur gradually. A firm will be in a much better position to do this if it already has at least some of the pull solution's infrastructure (see the top left-hand quadrant of Figure 5.2).

A functionally organized firm following the tightly integrated push model can start on the road to competitive agility by installing the collaborative infrastructure within the firm. Conversion techniques such as extracting and documenting business rules from existing systems (processes and application) for competitive agility are discussed in Chapter 7. The competitive agility and flexibility provided by the pull solution's technology infrastructure allow the members of the supply chain to add value to a customer relationship. This in turn helps the firm keep one step ahead in the effort to keep their product or service from becoming a commodity.

The Pull Model's Relative Impact on Service and Manufacturing Industries

On average, most firms in the services sector have less investment in PPE than those in the manufacturing sector. Therefore, the pull model is more easily implemented for services. As illustrated in the previous service chain example, the key to success is the ability of the trading partners to redesign and align their business processes to support the service delivery activities. Rapid adoption of the pull model is already occurring in the financial services industry. However, as pointed out earlier, investments in legacy information systems may also be specific to a particular way of doing business. A major impediment for some of the service firms in their move to the pull model is their existing investment in IT. Most legacy systems do not integrate well with the new collaborative infrastructure.

Service firms will be the first to notice the changing competitive landscape as new firms who are not weighed down by past investments in technology enter the marketplace. Consider the changing nature of services offered by firms supplying contingency staffing. A few years ago such companies would send temporary customer service representatives to solve a firm's staffing needs for call center services. Now, some staffing firms offer full-service call center management. Using integration technologies, the staffing firm can now support the complete task of staffing, managing, and providing call center services. This in turn allows the firm that is outsourcing the call center functionality to focus fully on customer needs without worrying about managing the call center. The staffing firm has extended its commodity service—providing temporary staff—to providing a full-service outsourced function. At the same time, the outsourcing firm can focus on its core value-added processes.

Manufacturing or the Knowledge of Manufacturing?

It will take a lot longer for firms in the manufacturing sector to adopt the pull model. In reality, it may be impossible for a firm that deals with tangible physical goods to move entirely to the pull model. Given that most forms of physical goods need a certain amount of time to manufacture and ship to a customer location necessitates that the supporting supply web have the forecasting and supply chain coordination capabilities provided by the push model. Efficient utilization of the PPE required to construct physical products will always require the functionality of the push model.

Firms that currently manufacture products are questioning whether their core competency is the knowledge of product manufacture or managing the physical assets to produce the product. Firms such as Nike that are focused on customer needs see themselves as specialists in product design and marketing, not necessarily in manufacturing. If flexibility and responsiveness are required, firms that are not invested in PPE have a competitive advantage over those that are. In the athletic footwear industry most competitors do not own their manufacturing facilities. Nike believes that its competitive advantage stems from effective supplier management and marketing skills.

However, some firms are valuing manufacturing assets and skills as a core competency. Consider the example of firms such as Solectron, which see themselves as custom electronic manufacturers and build PCs that are marketed under a variety of popular brand names. With the adoption of the pull model's collaborative infrastructure, manufacturing firms have to consider many new options of operating. Over time, some but not all firms may decide to pursue a strategy that is centered on knowledge assets about the customer rather than on the physical assets of production.

Integrating the Push and Pull Models

The concepts of pull and push represent two extremes of a continuum. As stated previously, very few firms will be able to adopt all facets of either model. Firms providing digitized products may be one exception to this rule because digital products can be customized in innumerable combinations with little added cost. Conversely, a few firms, ones with predictable demand for their physical products, will continue to focus on being the lowest-cost producer; some commodities come to mind. In reality, most firms must incorporate elements from both models.

Depending on the location of a firm's product in the product life cycle, the firm may prefer one form over the other. During the growth stage, product availability is paramount to the firm. A pull model with the collaborative infrastructure will support the market share objectives of such a firm. Over time, however, as more competitors enter the market segment, eroding margins will force the firm to optimize the utilization of its productive resources. The focus will shift from collaboration to synchronization of the supply chain. Ultimately, the firm may choose to add some innovation to the product to define a new competitive space; it might also divest the manufacturing process to a low-cost producer.

Technology-fueled innovations are shortening product life cycles. A firm with an innovative product or service may have very little time to capture market share and enjoy high margins before competitors emerge. What are the choices available to a manager in this turbulent environment? What changes within the firm and across the supply chain are necessary to succeed in this environment? What technologies should a firm invest in to provide for competitive adaptability during this transition period? Chapter 6 addresses these questions in the organizational context. Chapters 7 and 8 answer these questions from the technology integration and selection standpoint.

C   H   A   P   T   E   R   **6**

Organizational Alignment

Much of the preceding discussion has been focused on the characteristic features of the input sources by manufacturing and service firms. Not only do these features have implications in terms of transaction volumes, customization needs, and associated sourcing costs, but they also require structural responses from the firm. Firms organize in a particular way to guarantee the most efficient and effective use of resources in the production of goods and services. The productive processes must be arranged in the proper order, and the support structures to ensure staffing, payment of employees, data management, and other aspects of administrative overhead must be provided.

Organizational units have relationships with each other to facilitate the productive process and the smooth exchange of related information. Some relationships are vertical while others are horizontal. A vertical relationship is defined by the degree of authority one organizational unit has over another. In some firms, a regional office may supervise the activities of a local marketing department. Horizontal relationships involve units of equal standing, such as sales offices in different regions. The relationships between the units may change when firms make new strategic choices. For example, a large multinational pharmaceutical and health care supply company decided to regionalize its operations by installing local centers of excellence. Gloves and other rubber products for the European market were henceforth to be supplied by the Belgian affiliate, whereas certain solutions for intravenous use were to be provided by the British subsidiary. These changes were primarily implemented to achieve economies of scale in each of the production facilities. However, as a result the local country headquarters—not only in Belgium and Britain but also elsewhere in Europe—lost their decision-making authority over their manufacturing facilities because production now had to be coordinated to supply the regional market.

Information systems and other technologies, reporting relationships, business processes, and the firm's strategy must be aligned for optimal efficiency. If any one of these elements is changed, structural adjustments must be made to the others. This is especially true when firms are rethinking what they will outsource and what they will produce themselves.

At one extreme is the firm that consists only of the customer interface, providing mostly marketing and sales functions. Amazon.com is a such a firm. Its Web-based customer interaction provides highly customized sales and marketing functionality to a variety of products and services. At the other extreme would be a firm that is fully vertically integrated and even extracts raw materials needed for production—the automotive firms of the 1920s that owned and managed their own rubber plantations for tire manufacture were firms of this type. Organizational structure defines formal reporting relationships, the grouping of individuals into departments and their relationship to each other, and the systems to ensure effective communication, coordination, and integration across departments.

The scope of a firm's operations clearly has implications for the complexity of its organizational structure, its business processes, and its management approaches. Generally speaking, more vertically integrated firms are larger. Thus, their hierarchies tend to be taller. Taller hierarchies are associated with slower decision-making processes and less flexibility. Less vertically integrated firms are smaller, with flatter hierarchies.

As we have seen in previous chapters, some inputs are more easily sourced from outside providers. Commodities and other standardized goods fall into that category. Other inputs—those requiring extensive customization, for example, or those for which the supply is unreliable—are not as easily outsourced. In such cases, firms sometimes find vertical integration advantageous to reduce the costs of searching for suitable vendors and of repeated contracting. The trend has been toward divesting activities that do not contribute to the core of the firm's operations. During the last 20 years, managers have been told to focus their firms on core competencies: activities the firm does especially well and that provide a competitive advantage in the marketplace.

The more a firm's noncore activities are outsourced, the more the firm needs to deal with a multitude of external suppliers. The focus of attention shifts from optimizing internal decision-making and production processes to managing external relationships—a much more difficult and often unpredictable task. Add to this the increased demands by customers that the firm be more responsive and flexible, and it becomes clear that organizational relationships within the organization and with suppliers must become more flexible as well. If the firm does not adjust the decision-making process and the way work is organized to adapt to changing market conditions, it is likely to lose its competitive edge. The concept of structural fit is old, but it is receiving renewed attention in light of the swift changes in the business environment.

This chapter first explains the principles of organizing for efficient operations, then discusses outsourcing and the types of relationships firms have with their suppliers. We also contrast the structural implications of the market economy model and the network economy model on organizing within the firm. Finally we look at some coordination mechanisms available to firms that provide the necessary flexibility to operate in the network economy.

Principles of Organizing for Efficient Operations

In the context of designing a suitable supply chain solution, we are most interested in the information attributes of the organization and its structure. We can distinguish between vertical and horizontal aspects of organizing. Formal reporting relationships and the design of departments are structural elements that define vertical relationships. Systems that facilitate interaction across departments enable horizontal relationships. It is particularly useful to look at the information properties of these relationships. A firm must be designed to encourage both vertical and horizontal information flows. If it does not, employees and managers will either have too little information to make good decisions or they will spend too much time dealing with information not relevant to their task in the organization.

Examples of vertical relationships are hierarchical referral, rules, procedures, plans, schedules, and formal management information systems. Depending on the amount of coordination needed, several of these linkage mechanisms may be used. Horizontal information linkages are designed to overcome barriers between departments. These linkages are very important, because as firms and departments grow, they tend to lose touch with what is going on around them. This is what Lee Iacocca discovered when he joined Chrysler:

> What I found at Chrysler were thirty-five vice presidents, each with his own turf. . . . I couldn't believe, for example, that the guy running engineering departments wasn't in constant touch with his counterpart in manufacturing. But that's how it was. Everybody worked independently. . . .
>
> Nobody at Chrysler seemed to understand that interaction among the different functions in a company is absolutely critical. People in engineering and manufacturing almost have to be sleeping together. These guys weren't even flirting![1]

Examples of horizontal linkage mechanisms are paperwork (memos, reports, or email), direct contact through meetings and committees, liaison roles, cross-functional task forces to address special problems, teams, and full-time integrator positions or departments. Unlike a liaison person, an integrator does not report to a particular department. An integrator frequently has the title of product manager, project manager, program manager, or brand manager. The integrator role is superimposed over the traditional functional structure of the organization. Thus the role facilitates coordination of the activities of multiple departments, such as product development, manufacturing, and marketing. A project manager sees that a project is completed on time, makes a profit, or achieves other project goals, but he or she does not have formal authority over other team members with respect to pay, hiring, or firing. Project teams are probably the strongest horizontal linkage mechanism. Teams are often used for large-scale projects or major innovations. They have a more permanent character than task forces. The need for horizontal linkage mechanisms increases when the environment and the market change rapidly. Also, some production processes—particularly those where the production technologies used are nonroutine and interdependent—require more coordination. Often the firm's goals stress flexibility and innovation.

---

[1] L. Iacocca with W. Novak, *Iacocca: An Autobiography,* Phantom Books, New York, 1984, pp. 152–153.

Formal organization design involves three activities:

1. Defining the work activities

2. Establishing the reporting relationships

3. Deciding the departmental grouping options (by activity, by output, by user/customer, or some combination of these)

As firms grow, departments are created to perform tasks that are strategically important to the company. The chain of command, that is, reporting relationships, is a line of authority that links all persons in an organization and defines the ultimate decision-making authority.

The first task of organizing involves the definition of work activities. As market conditions require increasing flexibility, firms seek to respond by focusing on their core competencies and by outsourcing noncore activities. In the extreme, so-called network or modular organizations have evolved. Consider Nike and Reebok:

- Neither owns any manufacturing facilities.

- Both rely heavily on a network of suppliers to provide them with their products.

- Both are engaged in design and marketing.

Even companies that have traditionally been highly vertically integrated, such as the automotive firms, are increasingly divesting themselves of some of their parts production facilities; examples are Delphi and Visteon. The following section considers how to define core work activities, how to decide what to outsource, and how to manage the outsourcing relationship.

Outsourcing, Core Competencies, and Business Networks

Since the industrial revolution, we have moved from the machine age to the information age. The organizational focus has shifted from capital-intensive industries, such as steel and automobiles, to information- and knowledge-driven industries, such as financial services, logistics, and bio-technology. When pursuing economies of scale and operational efficiency, firms must balance production capacity. Idle capacity is costly. Thus the availability of supplies has to be guaranteed, leading firms to vertically integrate backward. Desire for control over the sales and customer service processes may lead firms to vertically integrate forward into distribution. Such control over distribution is useful to guarantee full utilization of production capacity because sales efforts can be intensified through rebates and promotions if inventory starts to pile up. However, vertical integration imposes the costs of managing bureaucratic overhead and diverts managerial attention across a variety of different production processes. For example, consider some of the large pharmaceutical companies. These companies spend much of their resources on R&D activities, but they also manufacture and market the drugs once they have been developed. The activities involved are quite diverse, and obviously require diverse managerial talents.

With the shift to information and knowledge industries, capacity utilization is becoming much less important. The competitive advantage has shifted from the effective use of capital to the effective use of human resources. Unfortunately, many pundits lead us to believe that this shift is revolutionary, claiming that the efficient use of capital resources does not matter anymore. In reality, firms must balance the demands of innovative capability, flexibility, and customization with the efficient use of their resources. This trade-off results in the following questions:

- What strategy should we pursue?

- Which productive tasks should we perform?

- Who can perform the remaining tasks for us?

- How should we structure the relationship with the outsourcing partner?

Firms must assess their competitive environment, market developments, and their internal capabilities in deciding what strategic options to pursue. A firm that is uniquely able to develop and bring new products to market often does not have the capability to pursue efficient mass production of the same product. Similarly, firms specializing in efficient production methods may not necessarily possess the marketing research and product development talent to constantly innovate. Additionally, the technologies and business processes employed by firms focusing on efficient mass production are likely to be drastically different from those of innovative firms.

Given their resources and capabilities, companies decide on what productive tasks to perform. Consider our earlier examples. Nike and Reebok focus on product development, design, and marketing. They do not engage in manufacturing. Increasingly, the large automotive manufacturers are moving away from making automotive components such as instrument panels, window glass, etc., and focusing on product development, systems integration, and marketing.

Once the firm has assessed its capabilities and decided which tasks it wants to perform in-house, suitable partners for the remaining tasks have to be found. These tasks may be services to the firm, such as accounting, human resources management, and distribution or warehousing, or they may involve the production of raw materials or component inputs. Of course, if a suitable partner cannot be found, in-house production must be reconsidered.

Some of these services and inputs may be sourced through arm's-length market transactions; others may involve closer and more long-term ties to the partner firms. The structure of the relationship with the partner firms depends on the market conditions for the inputs or services that are being sought and on the nature of the service or input. In the case of automotive firms, many supplied components are highly customized by car model. To take full advantage of the product expertise of the supplier firms and to ensure proper integration of the component into the finished car, automotive assemblers and suppliers jointly engage in product development. Such a relationship clearly goes beyond a market exchange transaction. In sum, the goal is to minimize sourcing costs while ensuring reliable and high-quality services and supplies.

As IT has enhanced our ability to efficiently access multiple sources of supply, to measure a supplier's performance, and to schedule production and delivery across firms, the trend has been toward outsourcing many activities that are not central to pursuing the business strategy. As a result, firms have developed intricate networks of business relationships with multiple tiers of suppliers and downstream channel partners. In some instances, these networks may be transitory. Specialized firms may be assembled for the duration of a specific project and disbanded as soon as the project is complete.

A famous example of such a temporary network occurred during the development of the B-2 Stealth Bomber. Starting in the 1980s, a large number of subcontractors were assembled into a "virtual corporation," with all engineering and development specifications stored in a single database. The four lead firms in this endeavor were Northrup (Northrup/Grumman), Boeing, Vaught (then a division of LTV Corporation), and General Electric. Hundreds of other firms supplied additional parts produced to specifications. Northrup, the lead contractor, did not have the resources to pursue this project alone or with fewer partners, because of the diversity in specialized technologies and the sheer size of the project.

Vertical Integration or Outsourcing?

The choice of strategy, the industry, and other market conditions will dictate the degree of a firm's vertical integration—the scope of activities the firm performs along the value chain. Firms may choose to produce their own inputs if these inputs are crucial for the production process and if there is uncertainty about the supplies being available when needed. Backward integration into supplies can also enhance the technical capabilities of the firm. Also, the more of a product that is produced in-house, the better the ability of the company to control the product's quality. Generally, firms engaging in vertical integration backward are either forced to do so because of product characteristics or market pressure or they do so because they hope to distinguish themselves significantly from their competitors. Consider Cannondale, a maker of high-end mountain bikes. Although most U.S. bicycle manufacturers source their bicycles and components from manufacturers in Asia, Cannondale makes its own components and produces its bicycle frames in Pennsylvania. Management considers the innovative frames part of its competitive advantage, and does not want to make its designs available to its competitors, which could happen if Asian suppliers were used. Furthermore, Cannondale's management feels that the proximity of the manufacturing location enhances its ability to make design changes in response to changing market trends. In addition, the in-house manufacture of bicycle components such as customized brakes and handlebars is seen as an effective way to capture aftermarket revenues.[2]

Forward integration provides more control over the sales and distribution process. Independent sales agents, wholesalers, and retailers handle many competing products and have no allegiance to any one company's brand. They will push what sells and earns them the highest profits.

---

[2] M. Sloane, "Cannondale: A Company Built on Innovation," *The Journal of Competitive Cycling,* no. 1, 1995, pp. 7–10.

Unreliable sales and distribution channels may lead to costly accumulation of excess inventory and underutilization of capacity. In addition, bypassing wholesalers and distributors may produce a relative cost advantage over rivals by eliminating their profit margins and other associated costs of wholesaling and distribution. Thus, end users can be charged lower prices. Although it is not integrated backward into manufacturing, Nike with its Niketown stores is a good example of forward integration. Here the purpose is not necessarily to ensure reliable distribution of the products—the Niketown stores account for only a tiny portion of Nike's total retail sales. Rather the stores are part of the company's promotional strategy. They enhance brand awareness and are designed to facilitate premium pricing. Utilizing direct sales via the Internet is also an example of forward vertical integration.

Costs of Vertical Integration

Vertical integration boosts a firm's capital investment in the industry, increasing business risk. Capital resources are tied up and cannot be allocated to more worthwhile pursuits, such as the development of new products or markets. A vertically integrated firm also has vested interests in protecting its investments in technology and production facilities, resulting in slower adoption of newer technologies. Integrated firms tend to react more slowly to technological and market changes. Vertical integration also locks a firm into using its own sources of supply, which may over time become costlier than those provided by outside suppliers as market conditions for inputs and distribution services change. Vertical integration may also necessitate balancing capacity at each stage in the value chain. For example, the most cost-efficient volume in the production of windshields will be different from the most cost-efficient volume of automobile assembly. Producing below the minimum efficient volume increases per-unit costs. If the internal capacity for windshields exceeds the capacity for automobiles, customers must be found for the excess windshields—likely among the automotive firm's competitors. Finally, forward integration may call for radically different skills and business capabilities from those needed for backward integration. Managers of manufacturing operations need to carefully consider whether they can develop the very different skills associated with wholesaling or retailing.

Outsourcing

Outsourcing narrows the scope of the value chain activities a firm performs. A more streamlined structure fits today's tumultuous, fast-moving marketplace. Outsourcing noncore activities yields two advantages:

- First, it holds down the unit costs and investment needed to turn out new products rapidly.
- Second, it frees companies to direct scarce capital and human resources to where they hold a competitive advantage.

Often support services—such as trucking, catering, data processing, and accounting—are outsourced. Manufacturing firms may also outsource the production of components to facilitate more rapid product development.

Outsourcing makes sense when an activity can be performed better or more cheaply by outside specialists. Higher-quality or cheaper components or services can be sourced from best-in-world suppliers, who have considerable depth of expertise and innovative capabilities. However, the outsourced activity must not be crucial to the firm's ability to achieve a competitive advantage. In addition, a firm should not outsource an activity if doing so would hollow out the firm's core competencies, capabilities, or technical know-how. For example, if manufacturing technology and product development are closely intertwined, outsourcing the manufacturing may diminish the firm's ability to innovate. One way for a firm to guard against loss of control and protect its manufacturing expertise is by designing the production methods that its contract manufacturers must use.

Outsourcing may also reduce a company's exposure to risk, changing technology, and changing buyer preferences because firms can quickly seek out new suppliers with the needed capabilities rather than trying to adjust and retool internal operations. Firms are able to assemble diverse kinds of expertise speedily and efficiently. And, as we will see in the next sections, reducing the scope of a firm's operations also reduces organizational complexity, reduces coordination costs, and speeds up decision-making processes.

Choosing between Supplier Alliances or Market Exchanges

Outsourcing relationships may have many forms. Again, we need to distinguish between the types of goods and services procured. The simplest distinction is between commodities and customized components. Commodities—goods or services—can usually be procured from a wide variety of suppliers. Thus firms will choose to use multiple sources of supply so as not to be locked in to the delivery schedules and prices of a sole supplier. However, if the need arises, firms will be able to purchase such supplies in the open market. The degree to which contracts with suppliers of commodities are negotiated on a long-term basis depends on how essential the input is to the firm's ongoing operations. Many suppliers of commodity items provide value-added services, such as JIT delivery or even stocking supplies on the customer's premises.

In the past, many U.S. firms maintained arm's-length relationships with suppliers, granting them short-term contracts to supply items to precise specifications. Even when a company used the same supplier repeatedly, there was no guarantee of an ongoing relationship. Price was usually the determining factor for granting a contract. The threat of switching suppliers was a company's primary means of stimulating competition among its suppliers. Although most progressive companies have abandoned this practice, using short-term contracts or buying materials in the open market still has its place in purchasing.

Particularly in the case of components, but also for outsourced services, long-term supplier partnerships have replaced contractual, purely price-oriented relationships. Firms have found it advantageous to form closer relationships with fewer, yet highly capable, suppliers. In turn, these suppliers provide value-added services, particularly in the areas of R&D and product development, thus enhancing the ability of firms to respond to changing market conditions. Increasingly, automotive firms use their suppliers to provide entire modules of components that are then assembled in the automotive firm's factories. Instead of providing an odometer, the supplier will provide the entire instrument panel, customized to the precise specifications of the car's design.

Similarly, geographically dispersed manufacturing and service firms look to a single provider of contingency staff to serve the firm's needs. This allows the firm a single view of contract labor use across the firm. The contingency-staffing firm may provide value-added services such as contract labor utilization by product line, which can be fed directly into the cost accounting system of the contracting firm. This relationship can't be price-oriented, as the contracting firm has to take into account its own expenses in managing hundreds of small contingency staffing firms' invoices to get a unified view of contract labor use.

The Costs of Spot Contracts and the Costs of Alliances

The distinction between spot contracts and long-term alliances is important because of the associated implications for costs and dependency. The primary costs that arise when using short-term contracts to secure supplies fall into two categories: operational and contractual. Operational costs include items such as the search costs associated with identifying the appropriate supplier and assessing the supplier's capabilities to provide the needed items and to deliver on time. Other operational costs are inventory holding costs, transportation costs, and communication costs with the supplier. Some of these will be borne by the supplier and reflected in the price of the items purchased. Contractual costs include the costs of writing the contract, for example, the costs of legal help, and the costs of enforcing the contract.

Alliance relationships lower or eliminate some of these costs. For example, if the firm forms a long-term partnership with a particular supplier, search costs are reduced, because no subsequent searches are needed. Alliance relationships also feature value-added services, such as JIT delivery. Such responsiveness on part of the supplier partner is feasible, because forecasting data or even customer orders can be shared with the supplier so that production schedules can be adjusted as necessary. Alliance relationships also create dependencies because alliances are formed with far fewer suppliers than spot contracts.

Let's consider some examples. A spot contract will most likely be used for commodity goods and services or one-time transactions. Consider employing the services of a house painter. Most likely you will invite several painters to give you price estimates. You may even check some references. The painter will be chosen based on price, reputation, and availability. After the work is completed, the agreed-upon price is paid. Rarely will a customer maintain a long-term relationship with a painter for subsequent services, although a repeat purchase may be possible at a later date. The primary contracting costs in this transaction are the search costs associated with identifying the appropriate painter. A long-term relationship with the painter is only warranted if frequent repeat purchases will be necessary, in which case repeated searches may prove too costly.

Dell's approach to partnering with suppliers is a good example of an alliance relationship. For each of the components needed to produce a PC, Dell picks one or two suppliers that are leaders in their specialty. Overall, the company attempts to partner with as few outside vendors as possible.

Dell prefers long-term supplier partnerships or alliances because that kind of relationship facilitates some of the integration needed to ensure JIT delivery of components, reliable supply even when there is a shortage of particular components, collaboration in product development, and scheduling and production planning.[3] Here the long-term relationship is required to minimize the potential for losses if high-quality supplies are not available when needed. Alternatively, to ensure maximum coordination in the production process, Dell could fully integrate into producing its own supplies. However, full integration by Dell into the manufacture of these supplies is not desirable, because of the cost advantages independent suppliers derive from technical specialization and economies of scale in production.

Although forming alliances reduces coordination costs, it also entails some problems. Reducing the number of suppliers makes firms more dependent on one supplier's reliable performance. Should an existing relationship not work out, it is time-consuming and costly to form new alliances. As suppliers and their customers form closer relationships, they may even invest in tools and equipment that are specific to their particular relationship, thus intensifying their mutual dependency. As long as both partners are deriving equal advantage from the continued relationship, no party will be induced to take advantage of the other partner. However, if there is inequity in the degree to which one partner depends on the other, opportunism may arise.

Coordinating Contracts and Alliances with Information Technology

Both contracting and managing alliance relationships have been greatly enhanced by IT. The business press has been buzzing with news about ecommerce and business-to-business exchanges. In general, IT enhances information transmission and data storage. Thus IT is an ideal tool for pooling the offerings of a variety of suppliers in a common marketplace, particularly for commodities. Such interorganizational systems have been used in the past to pool the offerings of a select group of participants, as in the often-cited SABRE airline reservation system. What is new is that Web technology and open standards, for example, extensible markup language (XML), enable more firms to participate in such exchanges more easily.

---

[3] Joan Margretta, "The Power of Virtual Integration: An Interview with Dell Computer's Michael Dell," *Harvard Business Review,* Mar.–Apr. 1998, pp. 73–84.

In terms of our earlier discussion, IT plays the role of a broker—it reduces search costs. Not only can firms more easily identify offerings in the market, they can also compare features and prices with a click of the mouse. The IT marketplace can also provide information about the characteristics of the participating supplier firm, for example, the firm's reliability. Firms may have to prequalify to participate in the exchange. Alternatively, information may be gathered on firms' prior performance and published in the electronic marketplace for all to see. Thus some of the other coordination costs, such as contracting costs may also be reduced.

Alliance relationships are also enhanced by the use of IT. In fact, it can be argued that the current wave of outsourcing and partnering between smaller and more nimble firms is partially driven by the ability to use technology to manage such relationships better. Proprietary systems have long been used between some suppliers and buyers. Wal-Mart's use of information systems to link its point-of-sale information with suppliers such as Procter & Gamble is an often-cited example.

Broadly speaking, there are two categories of systems linking alliance partners: systems that enhance transactions and systems that enhance collaboration. Most alliance relationships must accommodate both types. Such interorganizational systems provide a multitude of benefits. Most obviously, inventory can be managed in a timelier manner. In fact, Dell Computers does not hold any inventory to speak of. As mentioned earlier, Dell manages many long-term partnerships with select suppliers. Some of Dell's vendors have plants or distribution facilities within a few miles of Dell's assembly plants, and components can be shipped daily or even hourly to Dell's assembly facilities. Such responsiveness is necessary in a production system where the output is produced to order and product life cycles are extremely short. Using interorganizational information systems, Dell openly shares its daily production schedules, sales forecasts, and new-model introduction plans with its vendors.[4]

Vendors may also participate in R&D, product development, and engineering by using interorganizational systems to share data and drawings in real time. Less formal communications technology also enhances the quality and speed of staff interaction between vendor and customer. Early involvement of vendors in product development provides many benefits.

---

[4] Joan Margretta, "The Power of Virtual Integration: An Interview with Dell Computer's Michael Dell," *Harvard Business Review*, Mar.-Apr. 1998, pp. 73–84.

Product development processes are accelerated, because development can occur concurrently in-house and at the supplier's facilities. Although co-location of development staff may still be necessary, much of the interaction can be managed remotely. As a consequence, the "throw-over-the-wall" problem can be avoided, and the manufacturability of a design can be ensured. In addition, components will be of higher quality and fit better into the overall design.

Common standards for data exchange, such as EDI, have long been used. However, EDI systems are limited in their scope to transaction data. For richer information exchange, for example, the exchange of engineering drawings, firms have developed a wide variety of proprietary systems, even within the same industry. This diversity has important implications for smaller supplier firms. Smaller suppliers have more limited resources to invest in multiple proprietary systems to tie into the operations of their customers. However, it is in the interest of any firm to have as many customers as possible so as not to become too dependent on one particular order, and a supplier firm may invest in a customer's specialized information system in order to interact with the customer. The danger here is that once the vendor has made this investment, the customer may believe that the vendor is locked into the relationship and can be forced to make price concessions. The customer may threaten to withhold future orders, leaving the vendor to bear the costs of the IT investment.

A Network of Relationships

The development and dissemination of open standards, such as XML, will remove some of the costs and barriers to participating in alliance relationships. However, for the foreseeable future, integration challenges will remain, as firms are trying to adapt their existing systems to new partner relationships. Open standards will enhance firms' abilities to participate in network relationships. A true firm network will have many nodes, which can be assembled on an as-needed basis. Vendors or contractors will be able to flow in and out of the systems, depending on current market requirements.

For example, suppose a buyer for a clothing retail chain sees a beautiful sweater in a department store. She buys it and faxes photographs of it to contractors around the globe. In a couple of days, one contractor finds a factory in Indonesia that can copy the design. In a matter of weeks, thousands of replicas are shipped to the retail chain. Subsequently, the relationship between the retail chain, the contractor, and the factory in Indonesia is disbanded until the design and production resources are needed again.

Such a dynamic network structure is very lean, with almost no administrative overhead. All work activities are contracted out and coordination is facilitated by electronic means. For new firms, such a structure is ideal, because entrepreneurs can get product to market without incurring huge start-up costs. For mature firms, the network structure can reinvigorate product development without huge investments. In addition, network structures preserve and enhance the highly specialized capabilities of each individual node. Networks provide the ultimate in agility to respond to changing market conditions.

Networks are hard to manage because there is little hands-on control. Although networks do have a central node that initiates an activity, managers must adjust to relying on independent subcontractors to do the work. When many different subcontractors are involved, firms may experience quality problems. Sometimes, subcontractors raise prices once a company becomes hooked on their products or services. Problems may also arise if a particular network node is no longer available and cannot be replaced easily. Finally, networks may suffer from lack of loyalty and an inability to develop a corporate culture. Subcontractors are committed only to the task at hand because they may be replaced at any time in favor of a new contractor.

Both alliances and network relationships pose some additional management challenges. Typically, these relationships involve the interaction of teams from two or more partner firms. Team processes within firms are hard to manage, and when teams interact across firms, significant time and effort must be devoted to managing the relationships. The challenges fall into three categories:

1. Information access and exchange issues, for example:

- What information needs to be shared, in what form, and with whom?

- Where can information be found, how can it be efficiently shared, and who needs to be informed of updates?

- Who controls information access and how—while making information available to those who need it?

2. Communication process management issues, for example:

■ When many team members are involved, communication volume increases exponentially.

■ Who manages the communication between and among teams, and what triggers communication events?

■ Communication tracking is typically not available; thus new team members have no idea what has already been said and done.

3. Transaction management issues, such as:

■ Beyond order status, what is the transaction history? Are there cross- or up-selling opportunities?

■ What are the satisfaction levels by all partners? Are there any issues that need to be addressed, and by whom?

These issues regarding team processes in the interaction between partner firms begs the question of whether the traditional way of organizing productive processes is appropriate given changing market conditions. Internal structures may need to be changed to accommodate the richer nature of the increasing number of interfirm relationships that are being formed.

The preceding discussion elaborated on what issues to consider when defining which work activities to perform within firms and what to do with the remainder, as well as the costs and benefits of different types of partner relationships with vendors or subcontractors. We now return to the other two tasks of organizing productive processes, both of them internal to the firm. We need to understand the implications of increasingly dynamic market conditions for reporting relationships within firms and how to efficiently and effectively structure the relationships between the activities or departments that remain within a firm's boundaries. The following sections outline some of the structural options firms may pursue, depending on their strategic choices and market conditions.

Market Economy and Firm Structure

Under the market economy model, products and services are produced to forecasted demand. The primary focus of the firm's operations is on achieving economies of scale and economies of scope. Productive processes are arranged so as to optimize the utilization of production capacity. Thus accurate forecasting is essential. As firms grow from the entrepreneurial stage to having to deal with larger production volumes, division of labor occurs. In the 1920s Frederick Taylor highlighted the efficiency benefits of organizing divisions around similar activities; thus was born the principle of functional division of labor: a grouping of employees around a specific activity.

The functional structure is most effective when the environment is stable and the technology is relatively mature. Interdependence between departments is not needed. Organizational goals emphasize internal efficiency and technical specialization. The functional structure promotes economies of scale within functions. Co-locating manufacturing activities fosters capacity utilization, and co-locating employees promotes in-depth skill development. Planning and budgeting are very important in functional organizations. Cost reduction is one of the key goals within each function. The main weakness of the functional structure is slow response to market changes that require coordination across departments. Often innovation is slow, because each employee has a restricted view of overall goals. Pure functional structures, or silos, are most often found in small to medium-size firms. Figure 6.1 shows an example of a typical functional structure.

As stated in previous chapters, few firms employ only one type of organizational structure. Often, structural arrangements are supplemented with

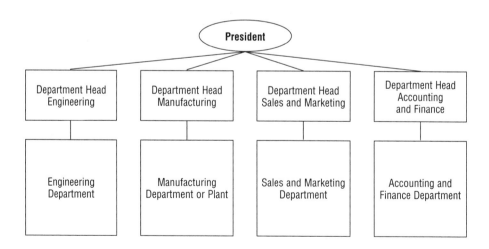

Figure 6.1: A functional organizational structure.

horizontal linkages. In today's uncertain environment, because of the need to respond rapidly to changing conditions, decision making along vertical channels in a hierarchy has proved to be too cumbersome. Most companies strive for flatter, more responsive organizations. To accommodate responsiveness, horizontal linkages are added to the functional structure.

As firms grow and become more mature, additional division of labor becomes necessary. Firms may either choose to organize around the customer or around different output (product) categories. Structures organized around the customer may be called geographic division structures. Structures organized along product lines may be called product division structures. Within each product or geographic division, functional departments are maintained. The main benefit of organizing around a product or a geographic region is greater responsiveness to market conditions. However, economies of scale in the functional departments are sacrificed, because functions are duplicated for each product or region. Integration or standardization across product lines or regions becomes difficult. For very large and diversified organizations, these structures are suitable because they push decision making closer to the market, into the product or geographic division.

Although product and geographic divisions are often evaluated on a profit-center basis, measuring costs and income, this approach is somewhat artificial because transfer prices for exchanges between divisions are not necessarily reflective of market conditions. As organizations grow, administrative overhead grows. In addition, despite attempts to supplement the structures with horizontal linkages, decision making becomes slow and sometimes bureaucratically and politically entrenched. It is easy to see that such lack of flexibility is inappropriate for highly volatile market environments. Managers are continuously in search of better, more flexible organization mechanisms while maintaining efficiency in the productive processes.

Network Economy and Firm Structure

As firms focus on innovation in a highly uncertain environment, the demands on the organizational capabilities change. Flexibility is of utmost value; economies of scale may never be achieved. It is clear that traditional organizational models are inappropriate for such conditions. Rather than organizing for maximum efficiency, the network economy model values the management of relationships. Because managing large organizations is cumbersome and expensive, firms seek to outsource noncritical activities. In the framework of formal organization design, we need to revisit the task of defining productive activities.

In the network economy, product requirements change so quickly that production toward a plan and staged inventory becomes difficult to implement; some items will be overstocked and others will be out of stock. Customization and flexibility become key. Firms must focus on activities critical to overall strategy. Advances in IT have enabled firms to gather and store more timely information about inputs, production, and distribution. In addition, collaboration with so-called strategic partners—often firms that perform outsourced activities—has become easier.

The need for flexibility requires additional horizontal linkages between the traditional divisions in a firm. Management of relationships becomes more important than scale of operations. As activities are outsourced, managers must ensure timely delivery and adequate quality, not just within their own organization, but also across independent firms, which is a much more difficult task. In the extreme, firms may resort to a matrix of responsibilities. Matrix structures focus on multiple outcomes, responsiveness to customer needs, and technological excellence. The matrix is a strong form of horizontal linkage, in which both functional and product (or geographic) structures are implemented simultaneously. The crucial difference between a matrix structure and cross-functional teams is that product (or geographic) and functional managers have equal authority over the team. The employees report to both. Figure 6.2 shows an example of a matrix structure.

Although multiple points of view facilitate achieving customer responsiveness and efficiency goals, decision making can be difficult and confusing. Participants experience dual authority. Managers and employees in a matrix-type organization need good interpersonal skills and extensive training. The matrix structure, however, is the most responsive structure to network economy conditions. Environmental and market uncertainties require extensive amounts of information processing and a high degree of interdependence between departments, vertically and horizontally. This arrangement is appropriate for medium-sized firms that have to juggle scarce resources, such as engineering talent, between multiple projects. Market

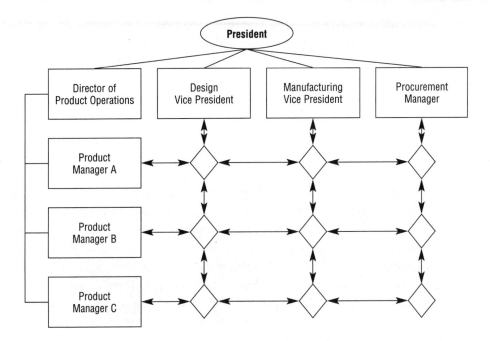

Figure 6.2: A matrix organizational structure.

pressure should exist for two or more critical outputs, such as technical quality and frequent product innovation. This pressure maintains the balance of power within the matrix.

Matrix structures and other structures emphasizing horizontal linkages also require that rewards and incentives for managers and employees be aligned with the requirements for information sharing. For example, in most companies sales staff are rewarded with a bonus or paid commission as a percentage of sales generated. To motivate a project team, including any back-office support staff, the entire team has to be rewarded based on the project's success. Unwanted side effects may occur. For example, undesirable competition for the same customer may arise between sales staff and customer service staff if customer service personnel are rewarded for up-selling and cross-selling. However, many companies miss out on up-selling and cross-selling opportunities precisely because there are no incentives for customer service personnel to generate additional sales.

Most difficult to solve is the question of how to organize and reward information sharing within and across firms. Today, in most organizations knowledge equals power and status. However, to be successful in managing a multitude of relationships with strategic partners or suppliers, firms must ensure that all relevant information is shared. Other information must be protected from leaking out to competitors through their relationships with their suppliers, as most suppliers also provide goods and services to competitors. To protect uncontrolled information flow, the number of contact points between the firm and its partners has to be limited.

Internally, employees must be encouraged or even rewarded for sharing information. Consider the following example from the consulting industry. Often, consulting firms use many independent subcontractors for specialized consulting tasks. These contractors may be specialists in a certain industry, or they may possess specialized technical skills. Obviously, the consulting firm will want to keep track of the performance of each of the subcontractors to weed out those who do not perform adequately. Project managers are usually responsible for assembling a team of consultants, including any required subcontractors. Therefore, there needs to be an information system providing project managers with information about available subcontractors. Upon completion of the project, the project manager reports on the performance of the subcontractor, providing others within the firm with the most up-to-date and relevant information about the subcontractor's skills and performance. In cases in which the subcontractor has not performed to expectations, the reporting task is fairly straightforward; although it will probably involve some paperwork (or data entry) on the project's manager's part, and a reward system may have to be put in place to ensure timeliness and accuracy of such reports. Given that project managers are generally themselves rewarded for completing their projects on time and within or below budget, they have little incentive to deprive themselves of the future services of subcontractors who have performed exceptionally well. Especially, in the case of scarce resources (reliable subcontractors are not widely available), the project manager may not want to praise the subcontractor too much for fear that he or she will become too popular. A conflict of interest arises between the project manager's goals that are only driven by the requirements of a specific project and his or her reward and the overall goals of the firm concerned with the optimal allocation of the best subcontractors throughout the firm.

Information Technology Solutions for Vertical and Horizontal Coordination

Within firms, a multitude of coordination mechanisms is employed. They are typically classified as formal or informal systems. Formal systems have evolved from paper-based manuals on policies and procedures and reporting and accounting systems. Larger firms have long ago computerized reporting, budgeting, and accounting. Thus information gathering and dissemination have become more timely and comprehensive. Formal systems primarily support the vertical relationships with an organization. In a large multinational firm, managers at headquarters can easily compile sales reports across all subsidiaries and get a clear picture of the company's overall global performance. At Mrs. Fields' Cookies, computer systems monitor hourly sales and suggest product mix changes, promotional tactics, and operating adjustments to improve customer response. Such transactional reporting systems speed up information transmission within organizations; in addition, embedded within them are reporting rules and procedures. Thus, depending on the strategic choice organizations make, decision-making authority within the organization can be more easily centralized or decentralized.

Informal coordination and communication systems are more important for flexible responses to changing markets in the network economy. The most prevalent of these systems is probably email, which has replaced the old paper memo. Other, more sophisticated technologies are also available, such as groupware. Historically, large corporations have always faced the problem of accurate and timely delivery of information within the organization and across the supply chain. Over the past few decades, the growth of multinational corporations has compounded the problem of outward information flow to the supply chain and divisions and branches and inward flow from branches to divisions and from branches and divisions to headquarters. A symptom of this problem is the inability of large organizations to present a single face to the customer. Information within such organizations is scattered across multiple functional departments (such as accounts receivable, order entry, accounts payable, etc.) and in most cases is not readily available at the customer point of contact.

To enable timely and easy access to company news, policies, policy changes, training, telephone books, and, most importantly, product and service pricing information; corporations have struggled with a variety of delivery mechanisms. Some of the traditional mechanisms have been printed newsletters, employee handbooks, price lists, sales guides, and training manuals. These traditional methods turn into logistical nightmares when the external environment in which the corporation has to compete is changing constantly. Once the costs of typesetting, printing, version control, distribution, mailing charges, and labor costs are factored in, it becomes apparent that the traditional methods of outbound information delivery are neither efficient nor effective. There is additional work for branches, which have to ensure that the correct versions of the price lists or policies are being used and provide for physical space to store the manuals, policies, and price lists.

Another major challenge facing geographically dispersed corporations has been how to facilitate collaborative work within the enterprise without having to gather people and files at a central location. Corporations needed a way to distribute staff expertise at the corporate headquarters level to the divisions and branches for collaborative work. In knowledge-intensive industries in particular—such as pharmaceutical companies and management consulting firms—immediate access to experts, and their participation in collaborative group work, are requirements for staying in business. Traditional methods of facilitating collaborative group work (for example, physically moving the experts to the needed location) are more expensive than ever.

Multiphase decisions within large corporations take a very long time. Major factors causing delay are the time taken for due diligence in each functional area and the need to share work files with other areas of the corporation. Traditional paper-based work-flow methods add greatly to the cycle time for multiphase decisions. The problems listed above have been solved over the years by software applications in the groupware category—such as Lotus Notes and Domino.

These types of systems provide a true flexibility to respond to changing markets because they support interaction across functions, often regardless of a person's rank in the corporate hierarchy. In many companies, CEOs encourage all employees to send them email to stay abreast of what is going on in the ranks. More importantly, email is used extensively to coordinate activities within and across project teams.

Email can be used not only to coordinate face-to-face meetings but also to accomplish substantial collaborative work, without ever having to interact personally. Project teams need no longer be co-located, as email can be used to share work in progress. In multinational firms, project teams can take advantage of being located in different time zones. Work started in Europe can be emailed to the United States at the end of the day. While the team members in Europe are sleeping, progress is being made in the United States. Bring Asia into the picture, and project teams can have 24-hour workdays. Moreover, email is also used extensively to interact with vendors and customers. Partners outside the firm can now be easily integrated into project teams. Such informal information systems enhance horizontal coordination within and across firms, thus clearly addressing the demands of the network economy model.

Compared to informal systems, which are quite flexible, large-scale transactional systems, with their built-in rules, procedures, and product specifications, can be a liability when trying to be responsive to new product introduction and new market conditions. A more modular approach to designing transactional systems is required. The business logic has to be separated from the transactions to allow for flexibility if requirements change.

Structural Flexibility for an Uncertain Environment

In summation, the network economy model requires intense coordination across multiple functions within and across firms. Such coordination is being facilitated by informal information systems, such as email. In addition, employees must be trained to work in teams. Horizontal coordination will, increasingly, be more important than vertical command and control.

The critical issues managers must address are which tasks to perform within the organization, which tasks to outsource, and how to manage coordination within and across firms. Once an outsourcing decision has been made, the relationships with the outsourcing partners have to be managed. Managing multiple external relations requires different skills and new types of coordination within firms. From a structural perspective, the activities remaining within the firms must be arranged in a way to allow for multiple perspectives to flow into the decision-making process. From the preceding discussion, two primary ways of organizing are apparent. Existing functional departments may be overlaid with project teams, or a matrix structure providing dual reporting relationships may be established. Either approach allows for more informed, timely decision making in response to rapidly changing markets.

Finally, reward and incentive systems must reflect the issues associated with information and knowledge sharing within and across firms. Traditionally, information has been associated with power. Cooperation between employees and across firms has to be ensured by controlling what information is shared and how. Systems have to be designed and incentives have to be provided to collect the unstructured information that is tied to horizontal coordination mechanisms. Equitable distribution of investments, revenues, and profits has to occur across the network of partner firms, as pure arm's-length market relationships give way to longer-term commitments.

Integrating Push and Pull Model Solutions

Few firms will find themselves faced with a pure pull or pure push supply chain system. Their product's position in the life cycle and their strategic goals will dictate the mix of pull and push systems that they need to compete in their particular market space. The organizational alignment and process changes described in Chapter 6 are necessary to successfully integrate elements from these two solutions. Without the alignment of organizational, process, and incentive structures, trying to integrate the two models will be like trying to mix oil and water. Superficial efforts may give the illusion of integration, but over time, the elements will separate into their original layers.

This chapter reviews the various technology options available for integrating the elements of the push and pull models within the firm and across the supply chain or supply web. In a majority of firms, IT professionals make technology infrastructure and application design decisions. However, selecting the appropriate technologies and high-level application designs are key to developing the competitive capabilities of a firm and its supply chain. We recommend that the technology selection and application design criteria for applications supporting the interaction between a firms, its customers, and its supply chain be made by non-IT managers, with IT professionals acting in a support role.

After completing this chapter the reader will have a better understanding of the organizational and process issues that must be addressed if implementation of integration technologies is to be successful. Integration technologies are reviewed with a view to providing managers a framework within which to make the appropriate technology decisions, given current and future business drivers.

Business Objectives and the Product Life Cycle

Most companies have multiple product lines. For each product line, the product's position in the life cycle will dictate the type of supporting supply chain systems. For example, the primary business objective of a firm with a mature commodity product is likely to be lean production. All trading partners in the supply chain are focused on efficient utilization of resources, with the overall objective of being the lowest-cost producer. At the same time, there is pressure from the firm's sales and marketing department to add features and functionality to differentiate the commodity product.

The mature commodity product's supply chain and firm will have become a lean production system through years of specialized investment in manufacturing equipment, synchronized processes, and enabling IT. Given the large number of specialized assets and processes involved in supporting the lean production model it is difficult for such a firm and supply chain to implement product differentiation features easily. In the past, this problem has been approached exclusively on the technology side: Information technology personnel attempted to implement a variety of solutions for integrating disparate technology platforms acquired over the years. However, the track record on replacing multiple technology platforms with an integrated technology solution for competitive agility has been poor.

A firm with a product in the growth stage will be looking for improved operational efficiency while attempting to capture market share. Often, new firms introducing competing products to the market have better operational systems than the early innovator. Even though the focus of the firm may be on product availability and market share, the firm has to incorporate the functionality from the push model supply chain solutions to remain price-competitive. The mixture of technologies to support this stage of the product life cycle may favor the pull model, but it must also have elements of the push model (from the SCP, SCE, or SCT areas).

Finally, a firm focusing on customer responsiveness by offering a large selection of product attributes may select a pull model for the customer interaction functionality. Upstream, however, sourcing, production, and delivery processes for direct raw materials and components prior to customization may be supported by push model technologies.

During the life span of a firm, it introduces new products, acquires market share, and then fights competitors as its products become mature. During this progression, a multitude of technologies and processes will have been put in place within the firm. Given the entrenched technologies and processes, it is a challenge for an established firm to remain competitively agile and bring new products to the marketplace.

Trying to replace disparate technologies of different vintages will distract a firm that is seeking to respond quickly to changing market conditions for its product. Instead, the focus should be on deploying functionalities (people, processes, and technology) to meet the competitive challenge at hand. A firm in the mature stage often has numerous SCE and SCT systems, supported by disparate technologies and processes, operating at a high and reliable volume. The manager's challenge is to leverage those areas that the firm has developed considerable expertise in, while facilitating new product innovation and competitive agility.

Categorizing Integration Technologies

Figure 7.1 shows an overview of the integration technologies available to support the sourcing, production, and delivery activities of a firm. For ease of exposition, they are depicted as *buy-side*, *sell-side*, and *in-side* integration technologies.

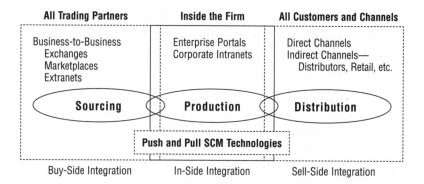

Figure 7.1: Overview of available integration platforms.

In terms of the reach and range chart shown in Figure 5.2, these integration technologies range from the top left to the bottom right quadrants. They allow customers and suppliers to perform a range of activities across the supply web, irrespective of their technology platforms. The activities involved may be as simple as sending electronic communications or as complex as processing transactions across disparate applications that are dispersed across the supply chain.

Innovation by software and hardware vendors aimed at providing integration solutions is growing rapidly—as are the accompanying technology acronyms. Despite the multitude of technologies in this area, it is convenient to classify them broadly as buy-side, sell-side, and in-side solutions. Using these categories together with the reach and range classifications in Figure 5.2, a manager will be able to map the level of integration functionality needed. We deliberately want to draw attention to the business functionalities of the integration technologies rather than to the specific features of those technologies.

Sell-side technologies provide customer interaction functionalities to a wide variety of direct and indirect channels. These may range from providing access to customers in an electronic marketplace to supporting retail and distribution outlets. Buy-side integration technologies provide integration for all procurement activities within a firm, including integration to MRO suppliers, direct raw materials suppliers, and electronic marketplaces. Some of the advanced integration solutions have functionality for virtual product development with the supply chain. In-side integration refers to integrating the multiple systems of record that a firm has acquired over its lifetime. By selecting the relevant level of functionality from these three categories, a firm can provide the infrastructure for competitive agility while selecting the mix of push and pull model features appropriate for that firm's product and strategic objectives.

In-Side Integration

Some of the major business drivers firms cite for wanting to integrate their internal systems are to:

- Support aggressive growth
- Allow geographically dispersed units to function as one entity

- Manage the information overload generated by huge amounts of data captured by multiple systems of record

- Leverage the investment in legacy systems

- Meet the challenge of increased competition

- Facilitate cross-organizational integration[1]

To capitalize on market opportunities and to support aggressive growth, a firm needs to redeploy its people, processes, and technologies. To grow, a firm has to have the ability to form multifunctional teams that can sense, satisfy, and enhance a customer's needs. Yet to grow profitably, the firm also needs elements of the push model to improve its resource utilization. Dispersed information that is stored in multiple databases across the enterprise must be turned into knowledge that can be used for cross-selling and up-selling. Developing this knowledge requires intra- and interorganizational communication of information.

We have already discussed how a firm acquires disparate technologies over many years. A typical time line may see a new firm acquiring a billing and accounts receivable system during its initial product introduction and growth phase. Based on sustained financial success, the firm may next invest in manufacturing systems. A growing volume of business and the launch of multiple new divisions may lead to new financial systems and a motley collection of other IT systems, particularly if growth occurs through acquisitions and mergers.

Following mergers and acquisitions, firms often plan to increase operating synergies by consolidating technologies with the merged firms. However, in most instances, it is difficult to consolidate the technologies, and the acquired firm continues to use its own collection of systems to conduct business. Anyone who has had to interact with various customer service departments has experienced a lack of integration across a firm's systems. Many times, customers are sent from one department to another, particularly if the problem falls outside the usual FAQs.

Consider a customer who has bought an appliance, is dissatisfied with the product, and wants a refund. On calling the 800 support number, the customer is referred to another department within the firm to get a return

---

[1]C. Hall, "Enterprise Information Portals: Hot Air or Hot Technology?" Cutter Information Corp. Report, Mar. 2000.

merchandise authorization (RMA) number. On inquiring why the customer service number can't help, the customer is told that the RMA systems and department are separate from the customer service group. Furthermore, the customer service department can't access that system, even though the helpful representative would have "liked to do that."

Such situations are common when customers deal with a mature firm, and making such a firm and its supply chain responsive to shifting customer needs is a very difficult task. Most importantly, before a firm can address the challenge of integrating the supply chain and customer interaction functionalities with the firm's internal systems, it needs to provide an integration platform for its inside systems.

Recall from Chapter 6 that the organizational and process alignment activities need to be coordinated with the roll-out of integration technology. Let's reconsider the appliance example. If integration technology allows the customer service representative to access and sanction the RMA number, training has to be provided to the customer service representative in the RMA process. Furthermore, RMA staff that previously held the responsibility for this activity needs to be redeployed. Finally, the way in which a customer service representative's performance is evaluated may need to be changed. If the representative is currently evaluated only on the time it takes to close a support call, other measures of customer satisfaction have to be added, such as problem resolution on first customer contact. Managers of the RMA and customer service departments will need to jointly manage and monitor the RMA process to make sure that customer service representatives do not recommend that customers return their products for replacement instead of trying to help them solve their problem using the product. This example highlights some of the numerous organizational and process issues that need to be resolved by managers when implementing integration technologies.

In-side integration requires two broad technology categories:

- Technologies that allow information aggregation and dissemination
- Technologies that provide the infrastructure to integrate transactions

The general categories of technologies that allow information aggregation and dissemination from multiple heterogeneous technologies are enterprise portals and intranets. These technologies map to the top left-hand quadrant of the reach and range diagram in Figure 5.2.

Examples of infrastructure technologies are enterprise application integration (EAI) systems and middleware technologies. These technologies, which map to the bottom right-hand quadrant of the reach and range diagram, provide the ability to perform transactions of varying complexity across disparate systems. There is a trend in the marketplace toward convergence of these and many other integration categories that have overlapping functionality. We anticipate that within the next few years, the distinction between information and infrastructure integration technologies will disappear entirely.

Intranets, Portals, and Integration Infrastructure

Figure 7.2 shows the basic architecture of an intranet or portal. Intranets have traditionally been defined as information aggregation systems and dissemination platforms. Over time, this functionality has been extended to

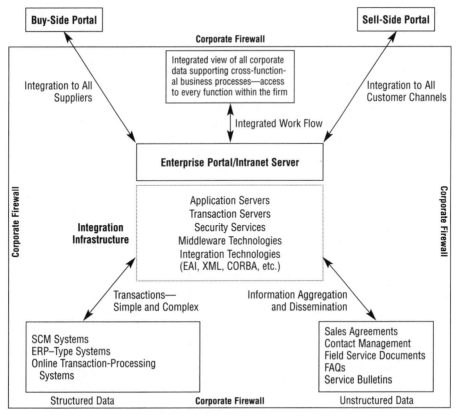

Figure 7.2: The basic architecture of a portal.

cover the ability to perform transactions across disparate systems. These more fully featured systems are also called enterprise portals. To keep it simple, we will use the term *portal* to refer to the information interface and to the underlying integration technologies.

Portals allow the integration of structured and unstructured data sources within the firm. This integration allows a firm to present a single view to its customers, its suppliers, and to its own staff. Functionally organized departments can use the portal technology to develop and implement business processes spanning multiple departments. This comprehensive functionality makes portal technology compelling. A review of the features and functionality provided by most transaction systems within a firm reveals that on average, an employee uses two to three screens within a single application to perform his or her daily operational tasks. As firms move to the pull model, tasks become more complex, and more screens and applications must be accessed. For instance, to fully support all potential customer requests, a customer service representative may need to use five screens from four separate applications. Through the portal server, these frequently used screens can be linked to support the natural work process of the employee. Depending on the portal product, the personalization module can allow the end user to modify and generate new work-flow linkages between structured and unstructured data.

Let us revisit the customer service representative example introduced previously. Suppose the customer service representative discovers that a new product is causing multiple customer calls with installation problems. The customer service representative may have used a series of screens from the RMA application, the service and installation guides, and order entry systems to solve this problem. The customer service representative now has the ability to share the problem-solving sequence of screens with the rest of the group.

This type of integration calls for a flexible and customizable infrastructure that can be modified regularly without intervention from the IT function. The integration infrastructure (shown within the dotted box in Figure 7.2) provides the functionality to ensure that transactions across multiple systems are completed in a secure and safe manner. In case of transaction failures, appropriate changes are made to all affected systems. Other important features include security, personalization, and work-flow management. The infrastructure layer provides the necessary features to integrate elements of the push and pull supply chain models within the firm. The integration infrastructure interfaces with the buy-side systems through SCT systems, which may consist of multiple online transaction-processing systems, factory automation, sales, marketing, and financial systems. These systems gather transactional data in operational data stores. To support the push model, SCP systems need access to information from these operational data stores for forecasting purposes.

Similarly, the customer-facing front end may have elements of the pull model—such as self-service and product configuration. As we saw in the previous customer service example, developing and implementing a single customer-focused process involves integration across multiple back-end transaction systems. The integration effort is significant and can lock a firm into a particular set of technologies. It is important to point out the role that integration infrastructure plays in integrating applications. Instead of investing in capable infrastructure, many mature firms have chosen to integrate applications directly. As a result, they have ended up with systems that resemble a tangle of one-to-one linkages between multiple transaction applications. Trying to integrate this tangled mess with added push or pull functionalities without an intermediate infrastructure layer increases the complexity of IT and decreases a firm's competitive agility. Putting in place integration infrastructure is a necessary step and lays the foundation for effective systems integration.

Implementing the integration infrastructure is essential not only to support the push and pull models, but also to allow the firm to replace aging legacy applications with minimal impact on ongoing business. As the infrastructure and interface technologies are put in place, employees can move from accessing the transaction systems directly to accessing them through the portal interface.

Over time, a firm may find that most of its staff is using the portal interface to perform daily operational chores. This natural evolution occurs because of the power the portal offers to customize the structured and unstructured data sources within the firm. Many employees have to log into multiple systems to perform their operational duties. If the portal interface reduces and customizes these multiple interactions to match employees' actual work flow, it has the compelling capability to change work habits. Through the portal infrastructure, the firm's staff is removed from actual contact with SCP, SCT, and SCE systems. Removing or implementing a new system will be transparent because direct interaction with the systems is minimized to a select few, such as SCP and scheduling staff.

Portal-type technologies are at an evolutionary stage. It is not as easy to implement the features as the previous examples suggest. However, despite their immature state, these technologies are addressing a problem that has plagued most firms since the introduction of computer systems. Firms have been generating huge amounts of data and have stored them in numerous systems throughout the enterprise, but they have neglected to incorporate contextual information and to provide comprehensive access for improved customer service. The enterprise portal provides the framework to solve this problem for both structured and unstructured data sources.

Mapping the various integration infrastructure technologies onto Figure 5-2 shows them spread out in the lower right-hand quadrant. Current examples of the available individual technology options are message-oriented middleware, application servers, and enterprise java beans (EJB). These names, however, don't mean much; new options, with different names, will have emerged before this book is published. Ultimately, the natural evolution of these technologies will see them all incorporated into portal-type technologies. Yet as portals are currently being implemented in firms, it is important to discuss the degree to which these integration technologies provide loose or tight coupling between transactions systems.

Transaction-Oriented Integration Technologies

Before we address loose and tight coupling of applications, let's review some of the currently available integration technologies. Note that the integration infrastructure shown in Figure 7.2 consists of multiple layers of transaction integration technologies. At the surface, there are business process integration tools that allow development of work-flow and transaction processes across multiple departments and systems. These business process tools map the work flow to underlying transaction systems. The lower-level integration technologies focus strictly on linking one system to another. These are typically point-to-point integration technologies. While lower-level integration technologies are relatively easy to implement, over time the accumulation of one-to-one connections becomes complex and unmanageable.

In the section on in-side integration, we mentioned a new class of integration tools called EAI. Enterprise application integration tool kits are meant to address integration of the business process layer and the system linkage layer. The core functionality of most EAI tools is the ability to convert data from one system and pass it on to a different system. In theory, the EAI platform acts as a universal data translator between disparate systems, allowing them to integrate. Although EAI tools are still in their infancy, they are rapidly maturing.

Most EAI tools use XML as the data integration language. Extensible markup language has been called the "lingua franca of the Internet" or "Esperanto—the universal language." The reason for XML's popularity is that it liberated data interchange between applications from the rigid requirements of EDI. With EDI, every data transfer between systems must be predefined and must conform to agreed-upon formats. This reduces the ability of interconnected systems and firms to react quickly to changing business drivers. In contrast, XML allows the exchange of variable-length, free-form text and highly structured data under the same umbrella.

Extensible markup language not only passes data between systems, it also provides information on how to interpret and process the encapsulated data. This is a powerful capability for EAI. As is the case with all visionary technologies, XML has yet to deliver on the promise of painless integration. A major reason for XML's failure to deliver is that standards are still evolving. Multiple firms and interest groups are trying to define these standards—from bodies such as Rosetta.net to EAI vendors. Despite the confusion about XML standards, the need for XML–type integration is great enough to cause businesses everywhere to push for widespread XML acceptance.

Varieties of other data integration technologies form part of the integration infrastructure. There are relatively mature integration technologies, such as remote procedure calls (RPC) and common object request broker architecture (CORBA). Newer integration technologies such as EJB offer similar integration capabilities across multiple platforms.

The transaction-oriented integration technologies enable services that are essential to coordinate the integrated flow of transactions across multiple systems, services ranging from transaction monitoring and processing to security, authentication, and personalization. The intricate mix of business processes and data integration needed to successfully build a single view of the SCP, SCT, and SCE systems results in significant technical complexity. This complexity, combined with organizational challenges, makes transaction integration a tough problem to tackle. One way for managers to make sense of this confusing complexity is to focus on the relative advantages of tightly coupled integration versus loosely coupled integration. The next section shows that by deploying loosely coupled integration, the process and organizational impact on individual departments can be minimized and the technical complexity reduced.

Loose or Tight Coupling?

When senior executives relay their grand vision of a system to the IT architects, it often sounds like this, "I want data available instantaneously at all customer touch points within the firm. Everyone should have real-time visibility into the supply chain processes and the state of the business." Unfortunately, this vision is used to drive systems architecture and leads to tightly coupled systems. Often, the underlying business need is not questioned. For instance, consider integrating screens from the order entry system and the SCE systems to generate a shipping date for a customer order. In a tightly coupled system, upon placing the customer order, the customer interaction screen is in a wait mode until the back-end processes check real-time availability of raw materials and production schedules to calculate the ship date.

A loosely coupled design can go through the order process without any wait screens. The customer receives immediate notification of the ship date calculated from batch availability data stored at the point of customer interaction. As opposed to direct interaction with back-end systems, a loosely coupled system is connected via asynchronous processes, such as batch updates, EDI, and XML feeds. What makes loose coupling superior to tight coupling? Loosely coupled architecture has the advantage of being able to generate ship dates with minimal technological lock-in to the back-end logistics and production and SCM systems. With loosely coupled integration, ship dates can even be received periodically from a contract manufacturer.

After order placement by a customer, the order information is distributed to the internal and external systems via loosely coupled mechanisms (EDI, XML). Loosely coupled integration reduces complexity and the degree to which IT assets within a firm are locked in to each other. Unfortunately, although integration decisions have a significant impact on a firm's competitive agility, IT personnel, rather than business managers, are usually charged with making these decisions. To enable successful integration while retaining competitive agility, business managers must thoroughly evaluate all options.

There are legitimate reasons for designing tightly coupled, real-time systems. Checking availability of finished goods in a warehouse for immediate shipment is a good example. Managers must be involved in the business process design phase and focus on the business need for tight versus loose coupling of the underlying integration infrastructure. This is essential to reducing the technical complexity of integration and the organizational impact on other departments.

As the number of real-time linkages (via tight coupling) to an application increases, the "owner" of the application—often a functional area—loses the ability to innovate within its functional domain. For example, the RMA area may seek to restructure its processes and technologies for greater internal efficiencies. However, the number of real-time links to their systems from other areas in the firm increases the complexity of rolling out their reengineering efforts. The roll-out will have to be coordinated with every "owner" of all the other directly linked systems. With a loosely coupled system, the department simply would have to ensure appropriate data feeds to all affected areas during the transition period.

Using loosely coupled systems, in-side technologies enable a firm to integrate (as dictated by business drivers) across disparate technologies without having to perform large-scale replacement of existing systems. Although some firms may require a fully integrated enterprise system to replace their collection of stand-alone systems, the decision to implement such a system should be made only after weighing the implementation risks and the competitive pressures facing the firm.

Factors Affecting Successful Portal Implementation

As discussed earlier, available technologies to support the integration of elements from the push and pull models are immature and evolving, and the technological complexities should diminish as the products mature. In the meantime, the common pitfalls to avoid when implementing enterprise portals are:

- Lack of clear business objectives
- Not allowing the users to own and define the process of personalization
- Treating the portal roll-out as a one-time event

- Treating the portal as a technology infrastructure problem
- Lack of a process to manage the portal
- Ownership of the portal

A firm considering portal implementation must have clearly defined business objectives for the portal. The high-level business objectives should be specific enough for the firm to be able to derive tactical integration initiatives from them. A business objective such as "integrate our business processes to participate in electronic business" may be a good vision statement, but it is not specific enough to ensure successful implementation of a portal. Examples of implementable business objectives are "allow an integrated view of historical transaction data from multiple systems of record to generate better sales forecasts" and "provide capability to perform financial what-if analysis for profitability at various forecast levels." Such objectives can be clearly translated into actionable and incremental steps for building a portal. Typically, $1 spent on acquiring portal technologies will incur a corresponding expense of $5 to $10 in technical services for back-end system and process integration. Therefore, having a clearly defined business objective narrows the scope of the integration effort and improves the chance of successful roll-out.

Users have to be actively involved in defining how the portal would be used within their normal work flow. Their role will be unlike their roles in any other system design activity they may have participated in previously. Normal system analysis for defining an IT solution involves a series of interviews with the users to determine what they need from the system. Prior to deploying the IT solution, users validate the planned system's features and functionality. Portal technologies, however, provide tools to personalize and customize work-flow features and provide access to structured and unstructured data. Unlike past IT solutions, which were static, portal functionality at the user end can be changed at the user's discretion.

Think of static IT solutions as akin to a bus route. A passenger is restricted to the predetermined locations on the bus route—there is very little flexibility on the number of stops or the amount of time spent at a stop. Putting in place portal technology is analogous to giving that passenger a car to meet his or her individual transportation requirements. The person can go anywhere, but the responsibilities and risks increase, the route has to be planned, and the person has to get a driver's license and insurance. Most importantly, the person has to know where he or she is going—otherwise, he or she might end up driving around aimlessly in circles. Initial user experiences with portals are similar. End users have enormous power and capability at their fingertips, but rarely use more than a few screens.

Given this flexibility, portal technologies can break down the information silos within a firm and allow an end user incredible reach and range. End users can create new functionalities within the portal environment without the need for IT resources. Unlike a transaction-oriented system for sales or accounts receivable management, portals aggregate data within the firm to create knowledge. This knowledge must be used within the proper context and made part of the daily operations of the firm. Because this is a dynamic and ongoing process, it needs the active participation of the end user. Without real understanding and commitment from end users, portal technologies will rarely deliver on their promise.

Portal roll-out and implementation are not one-time events, nor do they comprise a technology infrastructure project. The process is ongoing, and a governance structure is needed to manage it. In addition, the process for maintaining the portal and its ownership issues needs to be well defined. Because the portal provides the technological capability to break down functional boundaries (and accompanying stand-alone systems) within a firm, the impact on existing organizational structures needs to be carefully considered. A governance structure must be implemented to resolve any disagreements that may arise. By its very nature, portal technology is going to be at the center of many organizational politics. Without ownership at the highest levels and an appropriate governance structure, a firm might be able to use the technology to integrate push and pull models, but the technology will fail to deliver the requisite business benefits.

Buy-Side Integration

It is important to understand that without in-side integration, SCM systems from the pull and push models will be unable to deliver on their promise. The buy-side, or supplier, portal acts as a conduit for aggregating the various interfaces necessary to procure the entire range of products and services that the firm needs, from office supplies to MRO to direct raw materials.

Firms may consider implementing just one portal to serve both the in-side and buy-side integration needs. However, given the entirely different requirements for these areas (in terms of reach and range), it is essential to keep them separate. The buy-side portal will integrate not only the procurement functionalities but also the in-side and sell-side portals to present a single seamless view to suppliers, customers, and the firm.

Figure 7.3 depicts the various functionalities that the buy-side/supplier portal integrates. The firm has a single integration point for all its suppliers. Over the years, a typical firm develops multiple links with many suppliers. These links may range from tightly integrated applications to loosely coupled EDI links. On the reach and range continuum (Figure 5.2), these links would be depicted along the axis that runs from the top left-hand corner to the bottom right-hand corner.

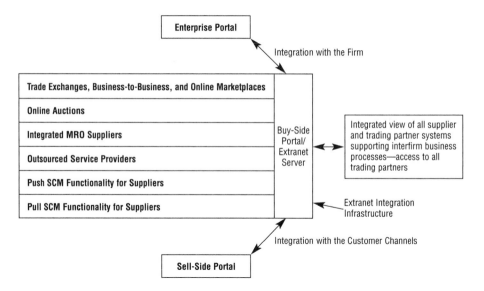

Figure 7.3: Architecture of the buy-side/supplier portal.

Adding to the complexity of buy-side/supplier portals is the need to have access to catalog and transactions systems of multiple suppliers. A purchasing specialist may need to sign into 10 or more different systems, depending on the item being procured. Integrating all the supplier links through a portal provides the firm with a consolidated view of the total procurement activities across the firm. Such a consolidated view is required to support a firm's ability to make strategic sourcing, manufacturing, and delivery decisions. For example, a requisitioner may select products from an integrated catalog. If the item being requested is not available in any of the catalogs, the portal procures the item from the best source, given factors such as timing, quality, and cost. The item may be procured from a marketplace, an auction, or from an external catalog source. Prior to using the supplier portal, the requisitioner may have had to go individually to external catalogs, Web sites, and auction sites to locate the optimum price and quality. Thus, for commodity and MRO items, the supplier portal greatly simplifies the interactions a firm has with its many suppliers.

For direct raw materials, the supplier portal can provide integration between the push and pull supply chain models. For example, a firm may place a certain amount of its product through indirect channels such as retail outlets. The rest of the product is built to order and sold directly to customers. In this situation, the firm may look for functionalities that support the pull model. The firm must communicate the customer order to the other members of the supply chain, check availability of raw materials, and promise a shipping date to the customer. However, this capability must coexist with the push model supply chain system. The supplier portal allows integration of pull and push functionalities where necessary.

As with in-side integration, firms can choose between loose and tight coupling with supplier systems, using EDI or one-to-one application linkages. Supplier portal technology allows a firm to consolidate hundreds of direct supplier links with the firm to a single point, reducing the information and systems lock-in that occurs with dedicated one-to-one links. Using a portal, a firm has the ability to seek alternative supplier sources, because it no longer has to worry about the IT integration aspect if it replaces a current supplier. This is of great strategic value, because it improves the firm's competitive agility.

Interaction with auctions, online marketplaces, and integrated MRO suppliers is built on technologies such as EDI and XML. Integration technologies supporting the pull and push supply chain functionalities may also include interfirm business process definition tools. To allow the supply chain to service both models, the demand signals from the indirect channels need to be fed into the forecasting model along with the pull demand from customers. The supplier portal allows for the incremental integration of pull functionality (such as customer self-service and product configuration) from the sell-side portal. With integration through a portal, the production systems are able to receive manufacturing releases combining the demand from the push system forecasts and the actual demand of the pull systems. Some SCM software vendors (who supply ERP packages as well) provide this functionality.

The best way to integrate the pull and push models is to introduce incremental functionality to support the firm's immediate business needs. For example, suppose a business needs to shift focus from optimal asset utilization to capturing market share for an innovative product launch. Given the relatively short competitive lead time a firm enjoys when launching a new product, installing the functionality to support the immediate needs quickly is paramount. Speed to market for the product, as well as installation of the supporting supply chain, are key to realizing market share objectives. In such situations, incremental, rapid, and reliable deployment of functionality is more important than when a firm is embarking on a major systems replacement effort. The portal provides the flexibility to quickly assemble the supply chain to support the new product launch. Of course, the suppliers' lead time to acquire raw materials and the inherent limitations of manufacturing lead times will still constrain the delivery speed to a customer. However, the portal reduces the time associated with communicating customer needs across the supply chain.

In contrast, a firm that started with a pure pull supply chain system may need to incorporate push system functionality as the product matures. In this case, because efficiency in asset utilization of all members of the supply chain becomes the business focus, the buy-side portal will have to provide tightly coupled integration for supporting the synchronized activities of the supply chain. The buy-side portal integrates with the in-side and sell-side portals to provide an integration infrastructure that allows a firm agility in its sourcing, production, and delivery activities, while reducing the integration complexities.

Sell-Side Integration

Sell-side portals provide the customer-centered functionality needed to support a pull supply chain. Irrespective of the channel of interaction a customer chooses—online, phone, fax, or mail—the sell-side portal presents a single place for the customer to interact with all the touch points across the supply chain. Sell-side portals offer a wide range of functionalities, for example, customized order placement and product configuration, account status inquiry, online self-service capabilities, and technical support. Sell-side portals can also be personalized to suit each customer's needs. The personalization may range from the look and feel of the screens to the types of information displayed for each customer.

The various elements of a sell-side/customer portal are shown in Figure 7.4 along with integration points for the in-side and buy-side portals. The customer can come to the portal directly, or be redirected from some other online place, such as an electronic marketplace or the Web site of a retail channel partner.

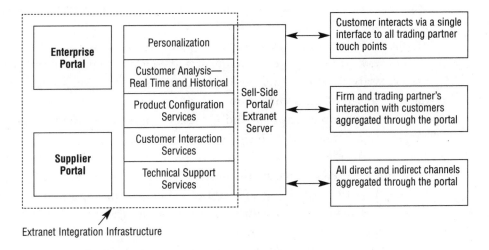

Figure 7.4: Architecture of the sell-side/customer portal.

Providing for real-time and historical customer analysis is an important component of sell-side/consumer portals. Historical customer data must be aggregated from the buy-side and in-side portal sites to intelligently suggest products or services that may enhance the total customer experience. Through effective integration, the sell-side portal presents to customers the appearance of dealing with a single entity. In reality, synchronized push supply chains and/or collaborative pull supply webs lie behind this uniform front.

Many vendor solutions, such as customer relationship management systems and customer portal systems, provide various levels of sell-side functionality. Selection of the appropriate technology for building the customer portal will depend on current and predicted customer interaction with the firm and the firm's existing technology infrastructure.

If a firm wants to direct more of its customers to self-service of highly customized products, product configuration and self-service modules may provide the appropriate functionality. These modules may need to be integrated with the buy-side and in-side portals to provide information on product availability and shipment dates to the customers. Conversely, if the business drivers point toward up-selling and cross-selling related products and services, the focus of the portal technology will be on customer analysis and integration with the in-side portal and historical databases.

Because customer experience with sell-side portals is so important to retaining the customer and enhancing the customer's experience, sell-side portal functionality must be rolled out incrementally, reliably, and speedily. Trying to do too much with unreliable software is likely to drive the customer away. At the same time, frequent and constant changes to the portal are necessary to attract and retain the customer's attention while staying one step ahead of the competition.

Far-reaching organizational and process changes across the firm and its supply chain are necessary to support any portal technology—in-side, buy-side, and sell-side. These challenges can be reduced over time if the portal technology is used to separate the business process rules embedded in applications from the underlying software code. This is an important concept, because it provides a firm with an application design framework that fosters competitive agility and leads to virtual integration across the supply web. In the next section, we will examine the role of business rules in information systems.

Business Rules as Competitive Enablers

Traditional software development practice was to give user specifications for an application to a programmer. The programmer then used the specifications to build a monolithic program. By "monolithic programs" is meant computer programs where the user interface logic, application logic, and especially business process logic are all coded together. These types of computer programs are difficult to modify in response to a competitive threat or opportunity.

Imagine building manufacturing plants in the same monolithic way. This would result in every plant having a unique configuration for raw materials delivery, production line, and shipping areas. Because building a plant involves tangible physical assets that will change over time, when building a plant, certain best practices are followed that allow for manufacturing flexibility. By contrast, over the last 40 years, monolithic IT applications have been developed and deployed across most firms without any business involvement in the actual architecture of the application.

When integrating systems across the entire supply chain or web, firms must code the business rules separately from the interface logic and the application logic. Thus, the rules can be changed to support ever-changing competitive requirements. Because programmers are not qualified to make business decisions for a firm, they should not be assigned this responsibility. We propose that subject matter experts from their respective business areas be involved in the development of application architecture.

What should firms and their partners do with the existing monolithic applications? How can they be integrated across the supply chain or supply web? Figure 7.5 shows how portal technology can be used for gradually separating business rules from the application and interface logic in existing monolithic applications.

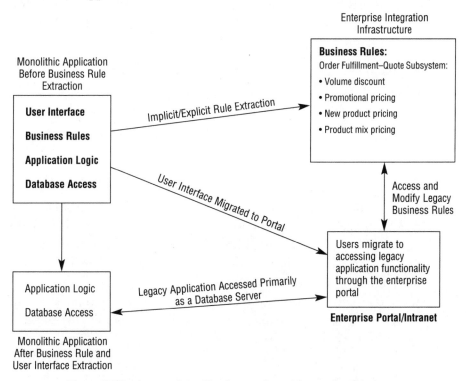

Figure 7.5 The integration of business rules with portal architecture.

User interface and application logic for existing monolithic applications can be incorporated into portals easily. An emerging class of business rule extraction software tools can monitor a legacy application to derive and extract embedded business rules. Using these tools, a firm can extend the life of its legacy application while adding competitive agility. While integrating elements from the push and pull models, a firm may realize that only a few embedded business process rules are needed to support its new SCP or SCE functionalities. Extracting just those business rules from a firm's monolithic legacy applications and providing access through portals immediately reduces the complexity of integration while improving competitive agility. Thus, replacement of all systems is not required and migration can occur as needed.

How to Choose an Integration Platform

The integration platform that a firm chooses for sell-side, buy-side, and in-side technologies is dependent on a firm's strategic choices, on the firm's business drivers, and on the existing information technology base within the firm. At the very minimum, an integration platform should provide the infrastructure for the following functions:

- Collaboration within the firm and across the supply chain

- Information aggregation and sharing from structured and unstructured data sources

- Business process definition within the firm and across the supply chain (work flow)

- Supporting transactions across heterogeneous disparate systems

Integration efforts may span months, even years, and involve numerous significant stepping-stones. Given the rapid evolution in functionality and features, the integration platform a firm chose at a particular point in time may not appear as robust as the latest offering in the marketplace. More importantly, it is difficult to foresee future competitive developments and their associated technology requirements. In this environment, managers must choose the most viable technology on the basis of current and likely future business drivers, the existing technology platform, and the technology vendor's long-term stability. The framework for selection of SCM technologies presented in the next chapter applies to the selection and implementation of integration platforms as well.

Selecting a Supply Chain Solution

How should a firm go about making SCM technology acquisition and deployment decisions? What is the recommended sequence of functionality roll-out? What organizational and business process alignment is required to successfully implement and realize the benefits promised by SCM technology? Specific answers to these questions depend on a firm's strategy and its unique competitive situation.

In this chapter, we present a general process that can be used by any firm to answer questions relating to the selection and roll-out sequence of SCM technologies. This high-level process specifies the essential elements that managers must analyze before a selection decision can be made. The focus of this chapter is on SCM solutions that are needed to source, make, and deliver a firm's products and services to its customers. Recommendations for procuring commodity items, MRO products, and allied services are discussed in detail in Chapters 2 and 3.

Recall the difference between push and pull model supply chains discussed in Chapters 3 and 4. The primary business driver for the push model is effective and efficient utilization of the physical assets of a firm, which may include factories, distribution centers, or retail outlets. Return on investment or similar ratios of sales revenue over invested capital are commonly used as indicators of efficiency. Minimizing the denominator of such fractions by increasing the efficiency of invested capital characterizes the push model approach. The pull model, on the other hand, is geared toward optimal utilization of the knowledge assets of the firm. The primary driver of the pull model firm is to use its knowledge about customer needs to create new sources of revenue and profit, thus maximizing the numerator of the ROI fraction.[1]

The primary focus of a firm—whether push model or pull model—will determine which of two very different technology infrastructures will deliver the desired optimization. This does not necessarily preclude a push model firm from being responsive to customer needs. However, the range of customer-responsive actions a firm with massive investments in physical plant can take is constrained by its existing investments. Similarly, while a pull model firm may seek to improve its margins, it will be restricted in its ability to make specialized investments in physical assets for operational optimization.

The push model requires technology to function as an enabler for effective utilization of PPE. This requires meticulous top-down planning to ensure that expected demand is forecasted accurately and that there is optimum utilization of resources across the supply chain. Examples of measurable outcomes from deploying push SCM solutions are reduced cash-to-cash cycle times and significant cost savings in areas such as procurement, manufacturing, transportation, and distribution.

In the pull model constantly changing customer requirements entail continuously destroying and remaking the value chain to produce the desired goods and services. A firm following the pull model uses its knowledge assets to direct the inclusion or exclusion of trading partners needed to service a customer's unique needs. The underlying assumptions here are that the push firm's product will have a lot of competitors and there will be substantial margin pressures, whereas the products of the pull firm are unique, with few if any substitutes. To avoid the margin pressures that come with maturing products, the pull firm may divest products from its portfolio once they acquire commodity-like status. The unique advantage of a pull firm is lodged in the knowledge assets that are used to continually innovate as customer requirements change.

The way that SCM technologies approach SCP in support of the push model is different from the approach for pull models. Planning in the pull model is a top-down exercise, where the production plan reflects the expected outcome. Feedback from the actual outcomes is incorporated into the plan-

---

[1]Adapted from G. Hamel and C. K. Prahalad, *Competing for the Future*, Harvard Business School Press, Boston, 1994, pp. 8–9.

ning process to change the production schedule for the next run. The pull firm provides a decision support environment based on actual conditions. In the push model, forecasters across the supply chain tend to be corporate strategists and senior management. Forecasting in push model firms is a formal, time-boxed, cyclical planning process; pull model forecasting is a collaborative, continual effort. As discussed in the previous chapters, no firm exclusively follows the pull or push model. Most firms incorporate varying elements of both models. In selecting SCM technologies, managers must be clear about the degree to which their firm is committed to either model.

The Selection Process

Functionality provided by push SCM technologies covers a broad range of SCP, SCT, and SCE execution areas. Pull SCM technologies provide functionality in the customer interaction areas such as real-time and historical customer analysis, self-service, and product configuration. Push SCM technologies range from integrated suites to point solutions, providing functionality in areas such as demand planning, advance planning and scheduling, and management of orders, materials, inventory, and transportation. The breadth and depth of push SCM technology solutions are significant.

Given the amount of organizational and process change that a firm and its supply chain have to go through, selecting and installing a technology suite that addresses all of the SCM areas are challenging tasks. The track record of ERP systems, which call for significant process and organizational change, has not been very good. Generally, the failures were not the result of poor technology; rather, the amount of process and organizational change needed to successfully utilize the technology was underestimated. Firms that were able to successfully implement the necessary organizational and process changes were characterized by strong leadership from the top. The necessary conditions to implement these types of changes were discussed in detail in Chapter 6.

Although in some cases "wholesale" installation of a fully integrated SCM solution may be called for; most firms should use an incremental building-block approach. Given the risks associated with implementing an integrated application suite and the importance of getting a product quickly to market, rapid, incremental implementation improves the chances of success and ensures that the organization and the business processes are aligned to support successful utilization of the technology. This generic approach can also be used for installing a fully integrated suite of SCM technologies.

Our approach to selecting an SCM technology highlights the importance of the competitive pressures, the firm's strategic choices, and the existing technologies of the firm and its supply chain or supply web. These three filters identify which facets of SCM can provide immediate benefit to the firm and have a realistic chance of successful implementation. The overall approach stages SCM functionality for incremental roll-out. Each successful implementation stage lays the groundwork for the next wave of functionality.

An overview of the roll-out process is shown in Figure 8.1. Note that the steps shown in the figure are necessarily sequential. Steps 1, 2, 3, and 4 can overlap or even occur in parallel.

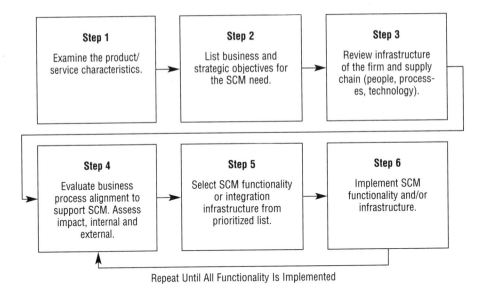

Figure 8.1: Overview of the SCM selection and implementation process.

Step 1: Product Characteristics

A preliminary step in selecting the appropriate SCM technology is to answer the following questions about each of the products for which the technology is being considered:

- Where is the product in the life cycle?

- If the products are at different stages in the product life cycle, are they currently supported by the same SCM technologies?

- Does the product share PPE and common components with other product lines that the firm manufactures?

A major challenge that a mature firm faces with its existing supply chain is the mismatch between the product and supporting supply chain technologies. Consider the example of a firm with a mature, commodity-type product. Such a firm must cope with a number of competitors and tremendous price pressure. To maintain market share and profitability, the firm has to adopt technologies that support operational excellence (refer to Figure 1.3). To enable the firm to be a low-cost producer, the deployed technologies must be tightly integrated.

What happens if the research and development department transforms the commodity product to an innovative one with few substitutes? Due to this innovation, the product would move from maturity to the growth stage in the product life cycle. This new position in the life cycle has great implications for the firm's strategic priorities. For the mature commodity-type product, the firm will have been trying to match supply to forecasted demand. For the new innovative product, the firm must ensure product availability to capture early market share and the associated higher margins.

If the supporting supply chain technologies do not address the needs of the innovative product, the firm will be left with unfilled demand or excessive inventories. Because supply chain systems focused on optimal asset utilization are based on detailed forecasting, they are ill-suited to deal with the unpredictable demand for an innovative product. In addition, a firm with an innovative product wants to capture market share rapidly before other competitors enter the picture. This requires that supply chain systems focus on rapid fulfillment of customer demand rather than on operational efficiencies. Clearly, a firm with multiple products all over the product life-cycle map will need more than one set of SCM technologies.

After identifying where products are in the life cycle and determining whether in-place SCM technologies support a particular product mix, managers must identify the shared components among the product lines of the firm. Common production lines and shared facilities must be considered. The quantity and variety of products a firm can produce is constrained by the amount of capital, labor, specialized manufacturing assets, and components. Assessing the product characteristics, along with shared PPE and resources, helps to ensure the alignment of the business objectives in the technology selection process.

Highlighting the potential shifts of products from innovative to commodity and vice versa before the technology selection process allows for the movement of products (and the value-add process) from one SCM solution to another without major disruptions in the operations of the firm. One outcome of step 1 is a mapping of the target products on the product life-cycle curve, including projected movements. The other outcome of step 1 is a list of shared components and PPE among the firm's product lines.

Step 2: Strategic and Business Objectives

Step 2 considers the role of strategic and business objectives in selecting a particular SCM initiative. Identifying these objectives is a more specific task than identifying the position of the product in the life cycle. The business objectives cannot be framed as high-level generalities; rather, they need to be specified clearly and concisely. Each objective should contain a goal (usually expressed in financial terms), and possibly a time frame. A sample of some clearly articulated business objectives follows:

- Enable market share growth from x to y percent.
- Reduce distribution costs to indirect channels by x percent.
- Increase inventory turnover by y percent.
- Reduce inventory-holding costs by z percent.
- Reduce logistics costs by $\$x$ dollars.

Evaluating business objectives in conjunction with the results of step 1's product life-cycle placement provides the necessary information to make a high-level decision regarding the type of supply chain for which the firm wants to implement SCM technology. But the business objectives may often drive additional, more fundamental changes in a firm's production process. In Chapter 3 we suggested that achieving some of the pull objectives may require a radical redesign of the production processes. For example, the business objectives may require that a product needs to be highly customized with delivery lead times of no more than 3 days. If the existing production process and supply chain cannot meet this requirement, the process must be changed accordingly. In this example, customization may need to be postponed until the very end of the manufacturing process. Only then, in conjunction with the appropriate SCM technology, can the firm pursue the business objective of 3-day delivery lead times.

These decisions need to be made by high-level managers well before any resources are expended on technology selection and implementation. Often, millions of dollars are spent by firms installing technology solutions before they realize that the technology will never deliver on the business objectives because of a fundamental mismatch with the firm's internal processes.

Step 2 also helps determine the mix of SCM (between pull and push) technologies needed to deliver the business objectives. Using the firm's strategic positioning for the target product, the mix of SCM functionalities can be mapped along three axes (Figure 8.2):

- Customization—predominantly pull model

- Responsiveness—push and pull models

- Lowest cost production—predominantly push model

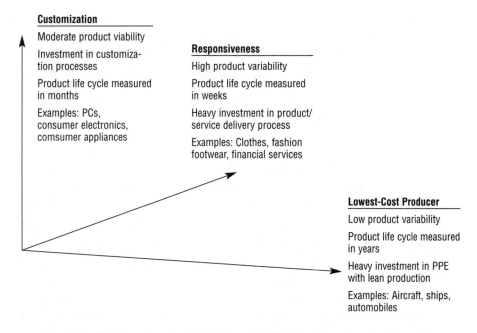

Figure 8.2: Mapping the mix of SCM functionalities in the push and pull models.

Any mismatches between a firm's strategic business objectives and the SCM technology options will be revealed in step 2. For example, if the firm views the product as being in the growth stage, but the business objectives emphasize operational efficiencies, there is a mismatch that must be examined and resolved before expending resources on the technology selection and implementation process.

If the firm intends to use customization features to reposition a product to the growth stage, managers must take deliberate steps to transition the existing SCM systems to accommodate the customization functionality. (Chapter 7 discusses how to integrate elements from both models.) Successful completion of steps 1 and 2 ensures the alignment of a firm's SCM business objectives with the product's current and future position in the life cycle, competitive environment, and supporting supply chain.

Step 3: Infrastructure Review

Critical factors for selection and successful implementation of a given SCM technology are the way a firm is organized, its in-place SCM processes, and existing ITs. There must be alignment between SCM goals and organizational realities if an organization is to be able to successfully use the SCM functionality. Consider a case in which one of a firm's primary SCM goals is responsiveness to customer requests within a certain time period. The firm, however, is organized along functional lines with multiple customer touch points across many departments. Without some form of organizational alignment along product lines aggregating the customer touch points, it would be impossible to realize the benefits of an SCM technology solution.

As we saw in Chapter 6, changing a functional firm to focus along product lines and emphasize customer responsiveness is not a trivial task. However, armed with the specific findings developed in steps 1 and 2, and a clear idea of the potential benefits from proper deployment of SCM technology, a manager is in a better position to make the case for organizational realignment to support the technology investment. Step 3 highlights the amount of organizational change required to support the functionalities of an SCM technology solution. The extent of organizational change and the functionality of the SCM technology that can be implemented must be mutually adjusted so that both remain in alignment. Managers may have to rethink which specific features of the SCM technology to implement.

An issue related to organizational alignment is change in business processes. Does the firm have a high-level map of core business processes within the firm and across its supply chain? The first time that managers in a mature firm look at business process maps they may be overwhelmed by the complexity of these processes. (Mature firms may not even have a clear process map.) Process maps must also indicate the role of the new SCM functionality in performing a particular function. A review of existing processes in the context of the organizational change and business objectives further narrows the technology options being considered. The process maps may reveal that implementing certain types of SCM functionality will require significant organizational and process changes that managers may not wish to address immediately. The high-level process map will become central to all supply chain and electronic business initiatives.

It is important to note that most SCM technologies have best practices embedded in them. Supply chain management systems, on the basis of industry best practices, dictate certain process elements for functionality, such as forecasting, scheduling, and logistics. To avoid complex organizational and process changes, firms may be tempted to customize the SCM technologies to fit their processes rather than change the organization. However, implementing the technologies by customizing them to fit the current organizational practices not only dilutes the chances of realizing business objectives, but also makes future technology upgrades difficult.

Supporting the process maps should be a detailed map of major IT infrastructure components enabling the process, including major applications (legacy and client/server), supporting databases, hardware, and network infrastructure. The high-level process and IT maps—which illuminate the integration from both a process and a technology standpoint—will help determine the set of feasible SCM technologies. These maps underscore the constraints from past technology decisions that limit the choice of future SCM technology decisions. They also serve to clarify the long-term transition objectives.

Using the methods described in Chapter 7, integration infrastructure technologies can help a firm overcome implementation limitations. The process and IT maps lay the groundwork for managers to prepare the case for installing the appropriate infrastructure to achieve technological independence and vendor neutrality. Particularly in mature firms with multiple heterogeneous systems, installing the integration infrastructure may be necessary to expand the choices of SCM technologies that can be considered.

Consider the following analogy: A firm would never design a manufacturing plant so that only one brand of conveyor belts and machine tools could be used on the factory floor. Yet most mature firms have installed IT systems that are locked in to one vendor's technologies. Mapping the processes and supporting technologies allows the firm to plan a gradual transition to technological independence from past process and technology choices. More importantly, mapping all the integration points within a firm's core systems makes it possible to outsource a process.

Evaluating SCM needs within the firm and across the supply chain, in the context of organizational structure, business processes, and the technology infrastructure, should generate a short list of feasible SCM technologies. Components of SCM functionality can now be aligned with necessary organizational, process, and technology infrastructure changes to support the successful implementation and use of the technology.

Suppose, for example, that a firm wants to improve the efficiency of its supply chain with business objectives such as faster inventory turns and cost savings in procurement, manufacturing, and distribution, and determines that SCP functionality will provide better decision-support capability to achieve its business objectives. A review of current processes and the heterogeneous transaction systems supporting them indicates that the data from the transaction systems needs to be integrated accurately before it can support the forecasting models provided by the SCP tools. Therefore, before an SCP solution can be considered, the firm has to ensure accurate integration of data from its transaction systems. The review, and the resulting process and technology maps, will be critical in narrowing the SCM technology choices for this firm and for highlighting infrastructure, process, and organizational dependencies.

As shown in Figure 8.3, the mapping process has the effect of filtering the SCM technologies, identifying infrastructure dependencies and sequencing them for deployment. At each step of the process, the set of feasible SCM technologies decreases while the chances of successful implementation and use increase.

Step 4: Assessing Impact on Business Processes

In step 4 the feasible SCM functionalities are rank-ordered according to their impact on business processes. To perform this assessment, a firm must further refine the high-level business process analysis developed in step 3,

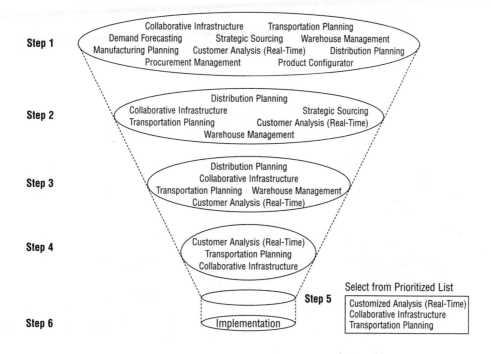

Figure 8.3: Filtering the SCM functionality set by business benefit and infrastructure readiness.

identifying what detailed changes will be necessary within the firm and across the supply chain to support the technology implementation. A given process change can be broadly categorized as incremental or radical. The impact of all process changes within the firm and on the trading partners must be assessed.

Once the impact of the process changes has been assessed, various integration technology options must be compared to determine the optimal method of integrating and deploying the selected SCM functionality with the existing systems—supplier, customer, and in-side portals. A detailed examination of the processes may reveal that an ERP system, with its integrated processes, is a prerequisite for realizing the process benefits from certain SCM technology choices. At that point, the business objectives established in step 2 need to be reassessed to see if there will be other benefits from having a tightly integrated process. Tightly integrated processes are not desirable for every firm. The need for tightly integrated processes should be determined after a thorough process review, balanced by a cost-benefit analysis. The manager's responsibility here is to guard against the natural bias of IT professionals, who may favor the technical elegance of an integrated solution. The non-IT manager must be convinced of the necessity for tightly coupled and integrated processes using the detailed process review. (Review Chapter 7 for a discussion of the advantages and disadvantages of loosely coupled and tightly coupled systems.)

At the conclusion of step 4, the firm will have a list of SCM functionalities and the processes needed to support them. This list also highlights the dependencies on other SCM systems and processes. Table 8.1 shows an example of such a list.

Table 8.1 List of SCM Functionalities and Their Impact on Business Processes

Functionality	Impact on Business Processes	
	Internal	External
Warehouse management	Minimal	High
Distribution	Moderate	Incremental
Forecasting	High	Moderate
Product configuration	Moderate	High

Depending on the immediate needs of the firm, these SCM functionalities may be broken down still further. For example, the firm may also require causal forecasting for which the impact on internal and external processes will be minimal. As mentioned earlier, visible and continued executive sponsorship is critical for implementing SCM technologies. Once the various functionalities and their impact on business processes has been assessed, it is possible to identify the right executives—those from the specific functional areas affected—from whom to seek sponsorship. A project has a greater chance of delivering on the projected business benefits if executives from the affected business process area champion the project. Step 5, the technology selection process, further refines the detail of the listed SCM functionalities.

Step 5: Selecting the SCM Technology and Infrastructure

In step 5, the output of the preceding four steps is considered, along with implementation risks and optimal executive sponsorship, and a list of feasible functionalities is prepared. In addition, managers must outline tangible and intangible benefits. There are three possible types of selection decisions:

- All the SCM functionality will be implemented as an integrated suite.

- There will be roll-out of a single application from the SCM area—for example, warehouse management or customer product configuration.

- The IT infrastructure necessary to support the SCM functionalities— integrated suite and single-application solutions—will be implemented.

Even if a firm decides to implement a suite providing integrated functionality in areas such as SCP, the roll-out still needs to be sequenced. This sequence will be dictated by the readiness of the infrastructure to implement the functionality. The impact on the organization and the supply chain of rolling out demand forecasting, manufacture planning, and transportation, distribution, and warehouse planning will be quite significant. When an integrated suite is to be implemented, the manager has to decide which features to roll out and in what sequence so as to balance the degree of change with the business benefit and infrastructure readiness.

If a firm decides that the greatest benefits will accrue from installing a warehouse management system, the firm may seek a best-of-breed solution rather than an integrated suite. While implementing best-of-breed single-category applications may be easier than implementing an integrated suite, doing so can create long-term integration problems. Integration problems will arise, for example, if the firm wants to add functionality in the SCM area, which requires integration to other features such as distribution planning.

To solve the SCM integration problems, a firm may decide to implement the technology infrastructures discussed in Chapter 7. Installing infrastructure first may allow the firm to expand the set of technologies it can implement while reducing the complexity of integration. By providing an infrastructure to achieve compatibility among its heterogeneous systems, the firm takes a first step to vendor independence and greater choice in the technologies it can consider.

Note that during the time it takes to implement a system, the output from steps 1 through 3 must be updated continuously with the most current business objectives. When the new system is rolled out, step 4 must also be updated, because the new system may have changed the old processes in ways that were not considered in the previous iteration.

Step 6: Implementation

As stated previously, we strongly recommend incremental and rapid roll-out of SCM technology or infrastructure. An incremental approach ensures that the technology components can be broken down into manageable chunks, thereby minimizing the degree of organizational and business process redesign that will be required. Incremental, rapid roll-out also reduces the risk of implementation problems that may arise if the competitive requirements change or new technology becomes available. Further, given the relatively short tenure of executives within the firm and across the supply chain, rapid implementation—say, within a 3- to 6-month time frame—will improve the odds of continued executive sponsorship for any given technology component.

In addition to adopting an incremental, rapid roll-out approach, there are many things a firm can do to facilitate implementation of the chosen technologies. The following general guidelines highlight some of the implementation pitfalls that a non-IT manager must pay attention to:

- Oppose any customization of the SCM technology with specially written code to support the firm's current processes.

- Insist on considering the alternative of procuring the SCM functionality from an application service provider (ASP)—should one exist for the technology under consideration.

- Keep the scope of the system from increasing beyond that determined in step 5.

If customization specific to the firm is required, it should be done outside the SCM technology. (See the section "Business Rules as Competitive Enablers" in Chapter 7.) This will lay the groundwork for a clean implementation that leverages the best practices embedded in the vendor software, while avoiding the firm's lock-in to a particular technology base. Many mature firms are locked into their technology base as a result of frequent and heavy customization to a particular vendor-supplied application. As a result, they are unable to upgrade to new versions of application software that may have improved or added new functionality in the SCM area because the vendor can't import the customized changes to the new version.

Typically, during the implementation stage the end users of the system request many modifications. They may claim that without those modifications they can't function. However, the IT staff charged with implementation does not have the necessary knowledge to challenge their claims or to suggest amending the process. In most firms the manager or executive sponsor in a particular area assigns a junior staff person to participate in the implementation of the technology. In most instances, however, the junior staff person lacks the credibility to challenge the end users on their stated need for modifications. As a result, changes outside the original business process are introduced. The only way for a manager to deal with this problem (given that a typical manager has a number of other ongoing initiatives) is to have a change control process that requires review and sign-off at the executive level—not at the staff level—for any deviations from the approved process. This will have the effect of limiting unnecessary modifications not relevant to achieving the business objectives.

Application service providers may be able to host the SCM application on their hardware and software and rent access to the functionality. If an ASP is available for the SCM technology being implemented, this option should always be considered first. It frees the firm from having to grapple with technology implementation problems, so the firm can focus on business process and organization issues. The internal IT department's role is simplified to one of providing access and integration points to the ASP. If the SCM project fails to deliver on its business objectives, it is relatively easy to extricate the firm from an ASP option and try an alternative SCM solution that may deliver the business benefits. Using an ASP is obviously not an option if a firm has chosen to implement integration architecture, which will be very customized and specific to the existing structured and unstructured data sources within the firm.

Finally, the non-IT manager has the responsibility to ensure that the scope of the system does not increase beyond what was originally planned. "Scope creep" is the leading cause for IT system implementation failures. Non-IT managers should manage scope creep with assistance from the IT professionals. Their leadership is necessary, because IT staff is not qualified to decide which additional requests are legitimate and which ones are gratuitous. Keeping these three pitfalls in mind—lock-in, scope creep, and failure to consider using an ASP—while rapidly implementing manageable chunks of the SCM functionality, will maximize the chances of successful implementation. Once implementation is complete, a firm can revisit step 4 to assess the impact of the new technology on the existing business process and to prepare the groundwork for selecting the next SCM technology. This incremental and iterative approach is independent of whether the technology supports the pull model, the push model, or a mixture of both. This selection and implementation process is based on software selection and implementation best practices developed over the years. The key to successful IT implementation and realization of a firm's business objectives is the alignment of business objectives and organizational and business processes with the selected technology. The recommended selection process is not only geared toward meeting the SCM functionality needs of a firm, but, more importantly, lays the infrastructure for integrating incompatible technologies within the firm. Over time, this infrastructure can free a firm from technological dependence on any one vendor's products. A firm must seek this technology independence for greater competitive agility and flexibility.

Consider the iceberg metaphor we introduced in Chapter 3 and revisited in Chapters 4 and 5. The process, organization, and technology solutions presented here directly address some of the visible and invisible avoidable costs. However, a large percentage of avoidable costs are associated with the scope of the firm, or the degree of vertical integration. We reviewed the reasons a firm seeks vertical integration in Chapter 6. Most of the avoidable costs due to vertical integration are hidden well below the surface of the water. We will show in Chapter 9 how the organizational structures, processes, and technologies that we have presented can be applied to remove the invisible costs of vertical integration. In that chapter we will also explain how to reap the benefits of vertical integration through virtual integration without the accompanying infrastructure lock-in.

Toward Virtual Integration

In the preceding chapters we presented the necessary organizational structure, business process alignment, and supporting supply chain and application integration technologies to reduce avoidable costs within the firm and
across the supply chain. For ease of exposition, we will use the term *enterprise infrastructure* to refer to the structure, processes, and technologies.
Deploying the enterprise infrastructure to support a mixture of the push and
pull supply chain functionality lays the foundation for a firm to move from
vertical to virtual integration.

We used the iceberg metaphor to show visible and invisible avoidable
costs within a firm and discussed the deployment of different enterprise
infrastructure solutions for reducing these costs. Another area that con-
tributes to avoidable costs arises from vertical integration. In this final
chapter we will discuss how the enterprise infrastructure that a firm deploys
to improve its supply chain performance can also be used to reduce the costs
of vertical integration. We will show how a vertically integrated firm can
benefit by moving to virtual integration. First, we need to briefly review the
enterprise infrastructure and its impact on other avoidable costs.

In Chapter 2, we reviewed the various type of goods and services a firm
procures and the various processes that occur within the firm. The types of
goods and services can be broadly classified as those that go into making the
finished product and those that are needed for administrative and maintenance purposes. Similarly, the value-added processes within a firm can be

classified as those that directly add value to the finished product and those in administrative and support roles. Close examination of the products that a firm buys reveals that the highest volumes of transactions are created while purchasing commodity and maintenance products. There are various technology and process options available for reducing the transaction and approval costs associated with purchase of maintenance items, and maintenance products, and administrative and support services are important categories to keep in mind when considering the organizational functions suitable for virtual integration.

The highest dollar value of purchases can be attributed to direct raw materials used within the firm. Not only do push supply chain solutions reduce the transaction costs associated with the procurement of raw materials but they also optimize the utilization of physical plant and productive resources within the firm. Pull supply chain solutions, on the other hand, are geared toward responsiveness to customers' needs. However, as we have repeatedly emphasized, very few firms will ever be part of a pure push or pull model. The organizational forms, processes, and technologies used to integrate these two models within the firm (in-side portal), across the supply chain (buy-side portal), and to the customer (sell-side portal) will serve to facilitate virtual integration.

What Is Virtual Integration?

To explain virtual integration, we first need to understand vertical integration. Vertical integration can be thought of as the activities that a firm performs in-house. These activities occur in the value chain processes that source, make, and distribute the finished product(s) or service(s). Other administrative and support activities, such as payroll processing, are also integrated for operational reasons. Firms concerned about availability may decide to produce their own raw material inputs. In the past, many large manufacturing firms owned their own power-generation facilities. Once power generation became a reliable commodity, these firms divested themselves of this in-house capability. *Backward integration* refers to traversing upstream in the supply chain to bring raw materials or components production in-house. Most firms use backward integration when they need to control a product's quality and availability. By contrast, *forward integration* provides more control over the sales and distribution process. Increasingly, firms are getting in touch with their customers directly, bypassing traditional intermediaries such as wholesalers, distributors, and retail outlets.

Virtual integration is based on the enterprise infrastructure, which provides the necessary mechanism for integrating a broad range of forward and backward activities within the value chain, including interaction with trading partners, industry networks, customers, and other maintenance and commodity suppliers. With vertical integration, the firm owns the productive processes needed to produce the raw materials and components. When moving to virtual integration, the channel master provides the necessary enterprise infrastructure to allow the raw materials or components manufacturer to integrate with the firm. As a firm moves from vertical to virtual integration, a department that previously belonged to the firm can become a supplier.

Consider the following example of virtual integration. A manufacturing firm spins off its distribution services into a separate entity. The new firm provides distribution services to the manufacturing firm through process and technology integration. To the manufacturing firm, there is no visible difference in the manner that it interacts with the distribution services spin-off. Order entry, manufacturing, and distribution processes are as tightly integrated as before the divestiture. The manufacturing firm retains some of the benefits of vertical integration without having to deal with distribution services ownership issues.

As long as the distribution services function was part of the parent firm, it had to compete for resources with other corporate functions, such as marketing, finance, R&D, and IT. Implementing innovative systems or practices within the distribution function in the vertically integrated firm can be difficult, because projects aimed at improving the distribution function within a firm may be far removed from the corporate mission of consumer product manufacturing, making it difficult to get higher-level executive support for those projects. As long as the distribution function is working properly, scarce corporate resources get allocated for other projects. Even worse, in times of economic hardship, noncore functions such as distribution services may be the first to face resource cuts.

The reality is that unless a function is strategic to the product or service a firm sells, it is very unlikely that the firm will allocate resources to make it the best in its class. The firm will be satisfied as long as the function is performed adequately and reliably. Once the distribution function is spun off, it can focus on its primary mission of excellence and innovation in distribution services. It can leverage its domain knowledge from the parent firm and enhance that with industry best practices to acquire and serve new customers and markets. The service level experienced by the parent firm will remain unchanged and may even improve because distribution-related innovations no longer have to go through the corporate bureaucracy for approval and implementation.

Virtually integrating distribution services is different from outsourcing them to an independent contractor. For starters, an independent contractor will not have knowledge about the parent firm's processes and procedures as they relate to interfacing with other functions in the firm. In contrast, not only does the virtual firm provide the distribution services, but the processes and systems are integrated in all functions within the parent firm—such as manufacturing, accounts receivable, accounts payable, etc. With an outsourcer firm, the service interfaces are clearly defined and the amount of customized process integration is limited. While this is good news for the parent firm, the virtually spun-off firm will have to develop a different model, similar to the outsourcer's model, to serve new customers. If done properly, this can be a win-win situation both for the function being spun off and for the parent firm. On the other hand, as we discuss later in the chapter, virtual integration can adversely impact the firm if it fails.

How Is Virtual Integration Different from Outsourcing?

The enterprise architecture allows a firm the necessary infrastructure to consider the outsourcing of various functions within a firm. This idea was introduced in earlier chapters as a benefit of deploying various portal-type technologies. It is important to distinguish between outsourcing and virtual integration. When a firm outsources a function, there is very little integration in terms of processes and systems. In the case of virtual integration, there exists significant process integration (enabled by technology) between two firms. The service chains previewed in Chapter 4 require collaborative processes across the trading partner firms for effective service delivery. The firms in the service chain have intertwined processes and systems for production and delivery of the service. A similar type of integration is required for two firms that are virtually integrated. The processes and systems between the virtually integrated trading partners tend to be unique, which supports process continuity across multiple firms. Knowledge about the former parent firm's internal processes and specific requirements from the virtually integrated functions is retained within the spun-off firm, enhanced, and shared with its trading partners. In contrast, in an outsourced relationship there is minimal knowledge sharing between the firm and the supplier of outsourced services. A firm that has outsourced a function or process has minimal process and system integration with the outsourcer. Consider the example of payroll, a function outsourced by most firms. A biweekly file is transmitted securely to the payroll-processing firm, which processes the information in the file and sends back a confirmation file. The payroll firm will be processing payrolls for many firms with multiple methods of reporting payroll activity such as hours worked, sick days, eligible vacation pay, etc. Despite the fact that these firms have different internal processes, the payroll firm receives a standard formatted payroll file from all of them. By standardizing the process, the payroll-outsourcing firm is able to provide a commodity service that can accommodate many different types of firms.

Let us consider a real-life example to illustrate the difference between outsourcing and virtual integration. Employees from an outsourced IT function for a health maintenance organization (HMO) were interviewed at various points in time during the outsourcing process—before, during, and after.[1] Before the outsourcing event, HMO employees could ask the IT function's assistance for things such as a minor report or modification and it would be provided promptly. After outsourcing, tightly written service level agreements (SLAs) dictated the nature and scope of IT services, and every request had to be reviewed to make sure that it was within the scope of the outsourcing agreement. The business users became increasingly frustrated because they kept hearing the words "out of scope" whenever they approached IT for a particular service. This could be viewed positively or negatively depending on the strategic value of the outsourced service to the firm. If a firm's business users are used to treating IT resources as a free commodity, outsourcing the IT function can be a good thing. A typical firm wastes internal IT resources on poorly defined automation efforts, for example, when an executive or manager calls on his or her favorite programmer or IT person to do a special project. These "special projects" have a way of snowballing and chewing up more IT resources when things go wrong.

---

[1] Kim S. Nash, "Outsourced IT Workers Feel Anger, Frustration," *Computerworld*, Mar. 5, 2001.

By contrast, if frequent and constant changes in a firm's information systems are needed for competitive or customer service reasons, outsourcing the IT function is a bad thing. In such situations virtual integration based on agreements that allow freedom to collaborate at the operations level are superior. A virtually integrated service provider does not have to operate under a strict SLA regime that dictates formal processes for every single request. At the same time, the service provider is compensated for ad hoc IT services provided to support the business. Certainly for the virtual services provider, a fixed fee contract with provisions to bill for incremental services provided gives the contracting firm the advantages of vertical integration without the associated costs of ownership.

Virtual integration has become feasible with Internet-based portal technologies. As we discussed in great detail in the previous chapters, portal integration technologies have the ability to integrate structured and unstructured data sources within the firm and across its trading partners to support an integrated work flow. Based on standards such as XML, these integration technologies allow structured and unstructured data from all trading partners to be accessed from a single interface. As illustrated in Figure 7.2, structured data sources are online transactional processing systems such as order fulfillment and accounts payable. Unstructured data sources are computer files with content about FAQs, contract terms, or field service manuals. The ability of the portal technologies to integrate processes and systems across the supply chain to build a seemingly integrated work flow to the end user will make virtual integration more prevalent. While these technologies are still immature, they are attractive because they use the incremental building-block approach. There are considerable organizational challenges involved in implementing virtual integration, and the building-block approach minimizes associated operational risks.

Figure 9.1, which is a slightly modified version of the reach and range diagram from Chapter 5, shows vertical integration, virtual integration, and outsourcing in the proper systems context. Given the technical and process challenges of completing complex transactions across multiple trading partner systems, the effort required to move a firm to total virtual integration is immense.

As we will show later on in this section, most firms will find that moving to the top right-hand quadrant will have diminishing returns given that the open systems vision has yet to materialize. High-volume transaction sys-

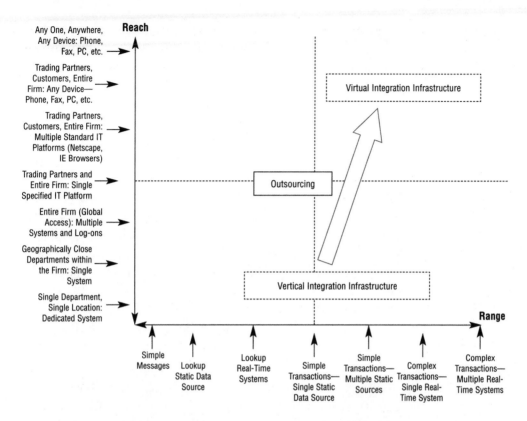

Figure 9.1: Outsourcing, vertical, and virtual integration infrastructure mapped for reach and range. Adapted from Peter G. W. Keen, *Shaping the Future*, Harvard Business School Press, Boston, 1991.

tem technologies are typically found in the lower right-hand quadrant of Figure 9.1. Despite technology vendor claims, from a process, cultural, and legal standpoint, it is currently impossible to build and deploy a single complex transactional system that integrates all trading partners and has global reach. (As discussed in Chapter 3, legal issues involve limitations on trans-border flow of information.) As a firm seeks to shed vertically integrated functions that are not strategic, it will follow a transition path along the arrow shown in the figure. Outsourcing requires minimal interfaces to existing transactional systems. Integration efforts may range from simple EDI feeds to real-time integration with a single system. Virtual integration, on the other hand, requires access to multiple transaction systems within the firm.

The fact that a firm is moving toward virtual integration does not imply the abandonment of vertical integration. Vertical integration will continue where it makes strategic sense for the firm. If a vertically integrated function has the ability to differentiate a firm's products and services and give it a competitive advantage, the function should be retained. Similarly, if there are concerns about reliability regarding the performance of a noncore function, it may make sense to retain that function. The trick here is that with the appropriate technology choices, functions within the firm and across the supply chain can be made to appear integrated. Using the virtual integration infrastructure discussed in Chapter 7, functionality from vertically integrated systems can be assembled to create a virtually integrated interface. True virtual integration will not be feasible, and may not even be warranted. However, the benefits of virtual integration in terms of competitive flexibility and agility can be derived from the appropriate infrastructure choices.

Benefits of Virtual Integration

Vertical integration functions are generally understood to relate to upstream and downstream activities in the procurement, productive, and distribution activities of a firm and in administrative support services. The biggest benefit of virtual integration is increased competitive agility. Like outsourcing or vertical disintegration, virtual integration liberates a firm from owning and managing assets and functions that constrain its choices. It is easier for a virtually integrated firm to move swiftly and capitalize on new opportunities than for a vertically integrated firm, which is usually weighed down by excessive investment in assets. Capital investments into noncore activities are cut, liberating funds for new strategic initiatives. Firms can also take full advantage of cheaper and higher-quality goods and services as they become available, which is not possible when internal sources are the only sources of supply. Virtual integration reduces a company's risk exposure to changing technologies or changing buyer preferences and enhances the firm's ability to assemble diverse kinds of expertise speedily and efficiently.

With virtual integration, in contrast to outsourcing, many of the advantages of being vertically integrated are retained. Most importantly, delivery schedules, production volumes, and design specifications are still developed collaboratively with the partner firms. Virtual integration diminishes some of the problems associated with outsourcing. Because integration of processes and technologies is maintained, quality control and potential coordination problems are mitigated. Effective virtual integration also allows a firm to rapidly increase its scale of operations in case of successful market penetration.

For instance, suppose a virtually integrated firm introduces a new product that is very successful. To meet the potential demand for its product, the firm has virtually integrated with an order fulfillment center that has specialized investments in processes and systems that are able to handle the unexpected load. Without the scalability provided by the partner, the firm might give an opening to a competitor while it was developing the necessary order fulfillment resources in-house. By virtually integrating, the firm has acquired the capability of integrating with the trading partners it needs to produce innovative products, as well as trading partners who can scale various functions needed to capitalize on market opportunities. The virtually integrated firm can bring on or drop trading partners as required to rapidly exploit a business opportunity.

Steps to Virtual Integration

It would take years for a mature firm to become a totally virtual enterprise—and it probably would not want to. Firms needs to carefully consider their options before spinning off vertically integrated functions. Consider the example of an electronic products firm that makes and markets home use products. The manufacturer may decide to spin off its manufacturing facilities and buy products made to specification from the virtual function. This may indeed give the parent firm temporary advantage from reduced costs, but in the long run it may have the unwanted result of allowing competitors to obtain and brand electronic products from the spun-off manufacturer. Or, worse, the manufacturer may decide to sell its own competing brand of electronic products.

No firm can ever be completely virtually or completely vertically integrated. Complete vertical integration and complete virtual integration represent two extreme ends of a spectrum mirroring the market and network economy supply chain solutions. A typical firm makes the move toward virtual integration by outsourcing certain commodity functions. Typical examples of outsourcing with minimal interfirm process and technology interaction are services such as payroll processing and accounts receivable collection. These outsourced functions require only standard, predefined file feeds in order to function effectively.

The requirements for virtual integration are more stringent. The firm that wants to become virtually integrated has to work closely with its trading partners. The collection of trading partners in a virtually integrated firm must be able to collaborate and support processes spanning multiple firms, but a customer interacting with a virtually integrated firm should not notice that they are dealing with multiple firms providing different aspects of product and service delivery. This requires well-defined collaborative processes spanning multiple firms. The organizational form and incentive structures across multiple firms have to be aligned to support the virtually integrated process. As discussed in Chapter 5, a supply chain community is a collection of virtually integrated trading partners that collaborates to capitalize on a market opportunity and disbands when it is no longer profitable to do so. Currently, limitations of organizational processes and technology make such a model extremely difficult to achieve. However the cross-functional and integrative organizational structures introduced in Chapter 6 are a step in the right direction. Given the difficulty of defining and implementing processes that cut across multiple departments within a single firm, the challenge of doing this across multiple firms is staggering. A firm can only outsource those functions that are standardized, such as payroll, or functions that are so well defined that they can be extracted with minimal effort from the parent firm. Similarly, to transition a function from vertical to virtual integration requires well-defined interfaces. Discovering and extracting the points of integration for functions to be spun off or to be virtually integrated are first steps in the integration process. Extracting and defining process and system interface points across multiple functions within the firm and across trading partners is not an easy task. To support virtual integration, processes and interfaces need to be clearly delineated. For example, the distribution function can't be virtually integrated if it encompasses both accounts receivable and accounts payable activities, yet many firms intermingle these functions for expediency.

The evolution to virtual integration will take place over many years, and will be propelled by competitors who do not carry the baggage of vertical integration for a given product or service. Theoretically, virtually integrated firms should have an advantage over vertically integrated firms when it comes to constant innovation in a product or service line. As we will see, a virtually integrated firm has its own limitations with regard to IT asset specificity that may reduce its competitive agility, just as investments in PPE reduce the competitive agility of a vertically integrated firm.

A Virtually Integrated Firm

Figure 9.2 shows what a virtually integrated firm might look like. In Chapter 3 we reviewed various options for reducing the transaction costs associated with procuring MRO and commodity items. We said that for a mature firm, virtual integration with an integrated MRO procurement firm would yield the most tangible benefits while minimizing implementation risks, and would free the firm to focus on strategic raw materials and supplier alliances, which have the potential for far greater financial benefits. Other services that can be virtually integrated fall within the administrative and support categories, for example, human resources, benefits administration, and call centers Most firms hire knowledge workers from consulting firms spanning business strategy to technology services. For many firms, these knowledge workers from consulting firms are an integral part of the corporation. Integration of knowledge workers and their parent firm into the processes within the contracting firm can be achieved through an out-side portal. Issues relating to performance reviews, availability, benefits, etc., need to be shared within the parent and contracting firm with different supervisors. The out-side portal can become the gateway for integrating service chains, as discussed in Chapter 4.

Figure 9.2 introduces the concept of an *out-side portal,* which refers to portal functionality needed by virtually integrated administrative and sup-

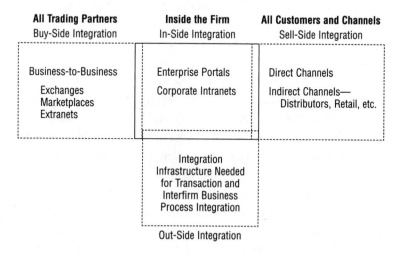

Figure 9.2: Out-side portal for virtual integration.

port services. The collaborative functionality needed for virtual integration has the same characteristics as those required for the service chain. The collaborative functionality needed to support the out-side portal is significantly different from the customer and supplier portals introduced earlier. The out-side portal functionality maps to the top right-hand quadrant of the reach and range diagram (Figure 9.1). The out-side portal has to provide the same degree of integration to structured and unstructured data sources within the firm as the in-side portal. For example, a firm may spin off the manufacturing function and focus exclusively on brand management. Conversely, a contract manufacturer may have only one internal function—manufacturing—with the rest virtually integrated.

Challenges of Virtual Integration

Unfortunately, virtual integration comes with its own challenges. A major challenge is that it requires process and organizational alignment across multiple firms. As we mentioned earlier, establishing process and organizational alignment is hard enough to accomplish within a single firm. The virtual enterprise will consist of a collection of highly specialized and focused knowledge workers from different areas—brand management, order entry, manufacturing, logistics, distribution, etc. Management challenges in such an environment abound. For example, who is the employee loyal to, the parent firm or the contracting firm? Setting in place the appropriate management and incentive structures to motivate a team assembled of outside consultants from multiple firms will be an extremely difficult task.

Extricating a firm from a virtually integrated process has its own challenges. Investments made in technology and process infrastructure will make moving to another supplier difficult. Extricating the firm from a virtually integrated process is easier than the divestiture of vertically integrated functions, but takes effort nonetheless. A firm will seek to integrate those functions it deems necessary for adding value in serving its customer as well as functions of strategic importance. Commodity product or service providers will find themselves in the role of an outsourced function. Virtually integrated firms will have interfirm processes and supporting systems exposing proprietary and confidential data to the virtual partners. A firm that exposes its proprietary data to another firm must not fear that the information might be used in the future for contract negotiations. Trust between firms is necessary before true virtual integration can occur. This will be the toughest hurdle to cross. Even if at the highest levels executives of the trading partners decide to trust one another, the reality on the ground will be different; that trust will not be easy to establish. For example, purchasing and accounts payable departments have traditionally viewed suppliers with distrust. In turn, there is no love lost from the suppliers, who have to make numerous phone calls to get their bills paid. Many functions that involve daily contact between trading partners have in the past had an adversarial relationship at best. This can't be turned around overnight by the CEO's mandating a new era of trust.

In many cases, vertical integration is necessary and beneficial. Consider the function of customer support during the launch of a new product. A firm may want to keep that function integrated and in-house until the product has stabilized. Keeping the function in-house gives the firm competitive agility in changing product specifications because the in-house call center can handle those changes immediately. Communicating, coordinating, and implementing changes across a virtually integrated firm takes more time than performing the same functions in a vertically integrated firm. Although this may appear to be counterintuitive, keeping certain functions vertically integrated during the product introduction phase allows competitive agility.

Taking into account industry conditions, a firm's strategic goals, and the technological feasibility of the available options, managers are charged with making the decision whether to virtually integrate or not. Virtual integration may not be appropriate for all functions. A firm has to make trade-offs between competitive agility and the relative costs and benefits of virtual integration. If the volume of transactions is not significant for a particular function—say contract manufacturing—a firm may not find any takers willing to provide the virtual integration. The cost of virtual integration given a particular transaction volume may even make a business line economically infeasible.

From Supply Chains to Virtual Integration

Over time the distinction between supply chain technologies and integration technologies for the support of virtual integration will become blurred. The typical mature firm has spent the past few decades optimizing its internal processes and its direct raw materials supply chain. As product and service life cycles get increasingly shorter, a firm will find itself moving between the push and pull supply chain models, and will need to look at various functions, at different stages, to decide whether the functions should be vertically or virtually integrated. During this important transition period, managers and executives will have to keep making technology, process, and organizational choices as they relate to their particular product or service. Deployment of flexible and extensible enterprise architecture will not only allow managers to provide the mechanism for moving between the push and pull models, but will also provide competitive agility through virtual integration.

The infrastructure discussed in this book allows a firm flexibility in deciding which activities to perform within the firm and in what form. Similarly, a firm has the ability to assemble a unique supply chain and virtually integrated functions that differentiate the firm from its competitors. The power of Internet technologies to disintermediate can never be the basis for sustainable competitive advantage. Given the low barriers to entry, any firm can easily replicate disintermediation for cost reductions. Assembling a unique supply chain, on the other hand, requires more than a technology or software package. It requires assembling the right combination of trading partners who can collaborate to give the channel master a secure and long-lasting competitive advantage. To paraphrase a business executive from the aerospace industry, "Supply chains and virtual integration are not IT challenges; they are, rather, corporate challenges that require intelligent application by business managers to change existing processes and organizational structures."

Sources

Achrol, R. S., and P. Kotler. "Marketing in the Network Economy." *Journal of Marketing,* 63(5) (special issue), 1999, pp. 146–163.

Al–Mashari, M., and M. Zairi. "Supply-Chain Re-engineering Using Enterprise Resource Planning (ERP) Systems: An Analysis of a SAP R/3 Implementation Case." *International Journal of Physical Distribution and Logistics,* 30(3–4), 2000, pp. 296–313.

Barry, J., J. L. Cavinato, A. Green, and R. R. Young. "A Development Model for Effective MRO Procurement." *International Journal of Purchasing and Materials Management,* Summer 1996, pp. 35–44.

Barua, A., P. Konana, A. Whinston, and F. Yin. "Making E-business Pay: Eight Key Drivers for Operational Success." *IT Pro IEEE,* November–December 2000, pp. 2–10.

Bradley, P., J. Thomas, T. Gooley, and J. A. Cooke. "Future Competition: Supply Chain vs. Supply Chain." *Logistics Management and Distribution Report,* 38(3), 2000, pp. 20–21.

Breen, B. "Full House." *Fast Company,* January 2001, p. 110.

Burns, K. "Manufacturing Logistics Reducing Costs." *Logistics Focus,* 4(9), 1996, pp. 2–4.

Cachon, G. P., and M. Fisher. "Supply Chain Inventory Management and the Value of Shared Information." *Management Science,* 46(8), 2000, pp. 1032–1048.

Chandler, A. D. *Strategy and Structure.* M.I.T. Press, Cambridge, 2000.

Croom, S. R. "The Impact of Web-Based Procurement on the Management of Operating Resources Supply." *The Journal of Supply Chain Management,* Winter 2000, pp. 4–13.

Daft, R. L., and R. H. Lengel. "Organizational Information Requirements, Media Richness, and Structural Design." *Management Science,* 32, May 1986, pp. 554–571.

Drucker, P. F. "Coming of the New Organization." *Harvard Business Review,* January–February 1988, pp. 45–53.

Dyer, J. H. "Effective Interfirm Collaboration: How Firms Minimize Transaction Costs and Maximize Transaction Value." *Strategic Management Journal,* 17(7), 1997, pp. 535–556.

Feitzinger, E., and H. L. Lee. "Mass Customization at Hewlett-Packard: The Power of Postponement." *Harvard Business Review,* January–February 1997, pp. 116–121.

Galbraith, J. R. *Organization Design.* Addison-Wesley, Reading, Pa., 1977.

Gilbert, S. M., and R. H. Ballou. "Supply Chain Benefits from Advanced Customer Commitments." *Journal of Operations Management,* 18, 1999, pp. 61–73.

Gilbert, S. M., and J. Sweat. "Chain of E–vents." *Informationweek,* July 26, 1999, pp. 18–19.

Hall, C. *Enterprise Information Portals: Hot Air or Hot Technology?* Cutter Information Corp. Report, March 2000.

Hamel, G., and C. K. Prahalad. *Competing for the Future.* Harvard Business School Press, Boston, 1994.

Harreld, H. "Pick-up Artists." *CIO Magazine,* 14, November 1, 2000, pp. 148–154.

Hendrick, T. E. "Purchasing Consortiums: Horizontal Alliances among Firms Buying Common Goods and Services What? Who? Why? How?" Center for Advanced Purchasing Studies, Focus Study, 1997.

Hess, E. "Building on an ERP Backbone." *Integrated Solutions,* October 2000, pp. 35–44.

Hess, E. "Open the Door to Information." *Integrated Solutions,* September 2000, pp. 29–36.

Iacocca, L., and W. Novak. *Iacocca: An Autobiography.* Phantom Books, New York, 1984.

Jahnukainen, J., and M. Lahti. "Efficient Purchasing in Make-to-Order Supply Chains." *International Journal of Production Economics,* 1999, 59, pp. 103–111.

Kay, E. "Working by the Rules." *Knowledge Management,* November 1999, pp. 50–53.

Keen, P. G. W. *Shaping the Future.* Harvard Business School Press, Boston, 1991.

Koch, C. "The Big Payoff." *CIO Magazine,* October 1, 2000, pp. 101–112.

Koch, C. "Four Strategies." *CIO Magazine,* October 1, 2000, pp. 116–128.

Kulkarni, S. "A Supply-Side Strategy." *Journal of Business Strategy,* September–October 1996, pp. 17–20.

Lawrence, F. B., and A. Varma. "Integrated Supply: Supply Chain Management in Materials Management and Procurement." *Production and Inventory Management Journal,* second quarter, 1999, pp. 1–5.

Linthicum, D. S. "Keeping in the Middle of Things," *Enterprise Systems Journal,* November 2000, pp. 34–38.

Magretta, J. "The Power of Virtual Integration: An Interview with Dell Computer's Michael Dell." *Harvard Business Review,* March–April 1998, pp. 73–84.

Monteverde, K., and D. J. Teece. "Supplier Switching Costs and Vertical Integration in the Automobile Industry." *The Bell Journal of Economics,* 13(1), 1982, p. 13.

Nadler, D., and M. Tushman. *Strategic Organization Design.* Scott, Foresman, Glennview, Ill., 1988.

Olin, J. G., N. P. Greise, and J. D. Kasarda. "Knowledge Management across Multi-tier Enterprises: The Promise of Intelligent Software in the Auto Industry." *European Management Journal,* 17(4), 1999, pp. 335–347.

Rosen, M. "Enterprise Portals," *Software Magazine,* 10–11, 2000, pp. 22–23.

Seideman, T. "Distribution for Hire." *Logistics Management and Distribution Report,* 39(8), 2000, pp. 61–64.

Shapiro, C., and H. R. Varian. *Information Rules.* Harvard Business School Press, Boston, 1998.

Slater, D. "Portal Potential." *CIO Magazine,* September 15, 2000, pp. 199–202.

Sloane, M. "Cannondale: A Company Built on Innovation." *The Journal of Competitive Cycling,* 1, 1995, pp. 7–10.

Stainbrook, C. W. "Integrated MRO Supply: Not Just for the Big Guys." *Supply House Times,* February 1998, pp. 45–46.

Strader, T. J., F.-R. Lin, and M. J. Shaw. "The Impact of Information Sharing on Order Fulfillment in Divergent Differentiation Supply Chains." *Journal of Global Information Management,* 7(1), 1999, pp. 16–25.

Supply Chain Council, PRTM ISC Benchmark Survey, 1997.

"Supply Chain Management: Benchmarks." *CIO Magazine,* October 21, 2000, p. 110.

Sweat, J. "CRM under Scrutiny," *Informationweek,* September 18, 2000, pp. 43–51.

Tapscott, D. (Ed.). *Creating Value in the Network Economy.* Harvard Business School Press, Boston, 1999.

Tyndell, G., C. Gopal, W. Partsch, and J. Kamauff. *Supercharging Supply Chains.* Wiley, New York, 1998.

Waters, J. K. "Portal Wars." *Application Development Trends,* September 2000, pp. 43–47.

Weill, P., and M. Broadbent. *Leveraging the New Infrastructure.* Harvard Business School Press, Boston, 1998.

Glossary

A

Application service provider (ASP)—Supplier offering a completely outsourced mechanism whereby the supplier develops, supplies, and manages applications software and hardware for its customers, typically with minimal impact on customers' internal IT resources—hardware, software, or personnel.

Arm's-length transaction—Business deal between independent and rational firms that are looking out for their own interests exclusively.

Availability to promise (ATP)—A technology providing the capability for a firm to check that it can deliver what it has promised to its customers. These checks go across multiple systems within the firm and across the supply chain to determine components and capacity availability.

B

Backward integration—Traversing upstream in the supply chain to bring raw materials or components production in-house. Suppliers of raw materials, components, and services are upstream to a firm. Raw materials and components flow down to the firm from upstream partners, where they are converted to products, which flow downstream through distribution channels to the customers.

Bill of materials (BOM)—A list of components that are needed to manufacture a finished product constructed in such a way as to reflect the manufacturing process aggregated at various levels. For example, on the BOM for an automobile there may be a component termed steering wheel. The BOM for the steering wheel will specify components needed for the steering wheel, such as the air bag, horn component, steering rod, and other steering components, in the order they need to be manufactured and installed.

Buffer inventory—Inventory consisting of raw materials and components that a firm keeps in reserve to meet unexpected or unplanned demands.

Bullwhip effect—Rapid and frequent changes in demand throughout a supply chain as a result of a particular event. For example, frequent increases or decreases in demand may lead to disproportional changes in raw materials availability in the supply chain. The further upstream a supplier is from a channel master, the greater the perturbation.

Business rules—Rules defining the way various functions are performed within a firm. For example, a business rule relating to discounts may state that any customer buying more than $5000 worth of goods will receive an automatic 15 percent discount.

C

Channel master—Among the trading partners in a supply chain, the firm that defines the processes for coordinated activity across the supply chain. In a computer manufacturing supply chain, the partner who brands and markets the equipment tends to be the channel master.

Collaborative system—A system, such as collaborative commerce, facilitating flow of information rather than processing of transactions. Using a collaborative system, business partners can exchange information such as inventory data by using a Web server as an intermediary. In many cases, collaborative commerce simplifies data interchange by eliminating the need for special client software at each customer's site.

Commoditize—A product or service that loses its unique differentiating attributes becomes commoditized. For example, the Sony Walkman when first introduced was unique with no substitutes. Over time many competing products were introduced, commoditizing the Walkman.

Commodity—An item the attributes of which are well known that is widely available from multiple suppliers. There exist many substitutes from multiple manufacturers for a commodity.

Competitive agility—The ability of a firm to respond to external threats or capitalize on opportunities by redeploying its internal systems—physical resources, people, processes, and systems.

Core activities—Activities that are central to achieving a firm's business objectives.

Core competency—Something that a company does well relative to other internal activities. Most retailers believe their core competencies reside in product selection and in-store merchandising.

Cross-selling—Convincing a customer to buy related items to the product under consideration. For example, if a customer is interested in buying a suit, a salesperson that persuades the customer to buy a matching shirt and tie has performed cross-selling.

Customer relationship management (CRM)—A comprehensive approach to providing seamless integration of every area of a firm and its supply chain that touches the customer.

Customer touch points—Any point at which a customer comes into contact with one of a firm's functional areas or a functional area of any trading partner in the supply chain. Examples of customer touch points are order entry, tech support, field service, and warranty claims.

Customization—The production of goods on a personalized basis to suit an individual consumer's tastes.

Cycle time—The time that elapses from the beginning to the end of a process or activity, for example, bringing to market a complex product or implementing an information system.

D

Direct labor—Labor that goes directly into making the finished product.

Direct raw materials—Materials used in the manufacture of a firm's end product.

Disintermediation—Cutting out the intermediaries in sourcing, manufacturing, and distribution transactions. An example of disintermediation is an automobile manufacturer that bypasses dealerships to sell cars directly to consumers. *Disintermediation technologies* facilitate the process of disintermediation by providing functionality that an intermediary previously supplied.

Disparate information systems—Heterogeneous information systems that can't directly communicate or pass information to one another without a translating technology.

Downstream partner—In the flow of goods and services along a traditional supply chain, a trading partner that receives the firm's output for further distribution or processing. Distribution channels are downstream to a manufacturer. Partners that are upstream to a manufacturer supply raw materials, components, and services to the manufacturer.

E

Electronic data interchange (EDI)—A set of specifications and associated technologies for electronically exchanging transaction-related documents between businesses. With EDI, in contrast to XML, every data transfer between systems must be predefined and must conform to agreed-upon formats, reducing the ability of interconnected systems and firms to react quickly to changing business drivers.

Electronic marketplace—Also known as an online marketplace, a marketplace in which Web-based technology makes it possible for the disparate systems of multiple trading partners to exchange and route business documents so they can buy and sell goods and services electronically.

Enterprise application integration (EAI)—The linking of applications, whether purchased or developed in-house, so that they can better support a business process. Most EAI software tools allow users to link heterogeneous applications within the firm and across the supply chain.

Enterprise resource planning (ERP) system—A single, integrated application that combines functionalities required by multiple departments in the manufacture, sales, and support of a product and enables the various departments to easily coordinate tasks and communicate with each other.

Extensible markup language (XML)—A data exchange format which, in contrast to EDI, allows the exchange of variable-length, free-form text, and highly structured data under the same umbrella.

Extranet—An Internet-based technology that links multiple systems within the firm and across the supply chain on private computer networks. Access is typically through a Web browser.

F

Firewall—Hardware and/or software which lies between two networks, such as an internal network and an Internet service provider and which protects the network by blocking unwanted users from gaining access and by disallowing messages to specific recipients outside the network, such as competitors.

Forward integration—Bringing in-house certain functionalities that were formerly performed by downstream partners, such as sales and distribution

G

Groupware—A technology that allows departments within a firm and trading partners across the supply chain to communicate, collaborate, and perform coordinated work-flow tasks.

H

HTML (HyperText Markup Language)—The standard of tags defined by the World Wide Web Consortium (W3C) to define how a Web page is presented in a browser. HTML is a subset of SGML.

I

Indirect raw materials—Basic raw material inputs that a downstream components manufacturer buys to build parts. For example, steel to be used in manufacture of automobiles is an indirect raw material.

Integrated suites—Application software that offers multiple features which span many functional areas within a firm. For example an integrated suite will have the breadth of functionality to handle processes such as order placement, fulfillment, billing, and other financial functions.

Intermediation technologies—Intermediation technologies consist of a wide range of Internet-based technologies (such as portals, EAI, groupware) that allows assembly of buyers, sellers, and other partners in the traditional supply chain in new and different configurations.

Intranet—A network that allows access, through a Web browser, to heterogeneous computer systems within a firm connected on private corporate networks.

Invisible costs—Costs that are not readily apparent, in contrast to visible costs, such as the direct purchase of goods and services. Examples of invisible costs are the costs of resolving a dispute and the costs connected with unplanned shipments.

J

Just-in-time (JIT) system—A process whereby suppliers deliver inventory to the factory just when it is needed for assembly. Just-in-time systems support communication between suppliers, making the as-needed ordering and delivery process feasible.

L

Loosely coupled information system—An information system in which the interfaces are well defined and data transfer occurs at discrete data transfer points.

M

Market economy model—A vertically integrated firm and its supply chain synchronized for optimal utilization of resources across the supply chain. The market economy model is geared toward "pushing" product to the customer based on forecasted market demand.

Maintenance, repair, and operations (MRO) item—A product that a firm uses to keep its manufacturing and operating facilities in good working order. Examples of MRO items are lubricants and replacement parts for conveyor belts; MRO items do not end up in a firm's end products.

Manufacturing resources planning (MRP)—A planning system that provides the tools for coordinating the efforts of manufacturing, finance, marketing, and engineering toward achieving the objectives of a common business plan.

N

Network economy model—A model in which the resources of a firm are geared toward allowing customers to "pull" products customized to their individual needs. In this model the firm and its network of trading partners are organized to meet unforecasted demand patterns.

O

Operational optimization—A focus on effective and efficient utilization of the resources of a firm to perform a particular function, such as manufacturing or distribution.

P

Point solution software—Limited-application software. For example, software that specializes in logistics does not provide functionality to other logistics related functions.

Portal—An application that integrates structured and unstructured data sources from disparate computer systems by providing access to these systems through a Web-based interface. Portals can perform complex and reliable transactions across multiple systems given the appropriate integration infrastructure.

Productive process—The term used to define all the transformation processes that occur within a firm. These processes take as inputs the entire spectrum of goods and services procured by a firm—direct raw materials, direct services, property, plant, equipment, administrative support services, and maintenance resources—and transform them into products and services that are used by the firm's customers, employees, trading partners, and other stakeholders Manufacturing or production processes are a subset of the productive process.

Property, plant, and equipment (PPE)—The physical resources that a firm needs for its productive processes and employees to source, manufacture, and distribute finished goods and services.

Pull model—The network economy model.

Push model—The market economy model.

R

Reach and range—Two concepts that together allow managers to evaluate various integration and infrastructure options. The concept of reach as it relates to IT infrastructure refers to the capability of the technology to allow interaction with other systems within the firm and across the trading partner network. At one end of the reach spectrum are dedicated systems; at the other end are systems that allow communication between all members of a network, at all points, using any device. The range of an integration technology describes the nature of the interactions the technology facilitates across the reach spectrum. At one end of the range spectrum is the ability to send simple messages; at the other end is the ability to perform complex transactions across multiple real-time systems.

S

Scalability—The ability of a business, manufacturing, or technology process to support sudden increases in demand.

Service chain—Process mapping and alignment across the trading partner firms enabling collaboration in the service production and delivery process.

Service level agreement (SLA)—A contract that defines the technical support and/or business performance guarantees that a trading partner offers its customers. The agreement typically spells out measures for evaluating performance and the consequences of failure.

Shelf life—The amount of time a product or service can be stored after manufacture. Shelf life for food items is low, whereas shelf life for some service items such as airline seats diminishes as it closes the boarding door.

Supply chain community—A group of firms each specializing in a particular area, such as contract manufacturing, order fulfillment, or logistics services, which collaborate to satisfy an emerging customer need. The trading partners within the community share the costs and profits in an equitable manner.

Supply chain execution (SCE) system—A system the focus of which is on reducing unplanned shipping costs and inventory holding costs. Applications to support SCE systems address areas such as warehouse management and transportation management.

Supply chain management (SCM)—A group of applications that execute sourcing, manufacturing, and distributions operations such as managing warehouses, inventory supplies, and distribution channels. There are three types of SCM systems: execution, planning, and transaction.

Supply chain planning (SCP) system—A planning system that takes the demand forecast for a product and uses it to specify how the product is going to be manufactured and sourced. It can be thought of as a decision support tool that allows what-if planning based on the constraints within the firm and across the supply chain.

Supply chain transaction (SCT) system—A system that records and integrates all information flows between the trading partners through supply chain management, supply chain execution systems, and other internal transaction systems.

Supply web—The network of supply chains that supports the pull model. Use of the word "web" conveys the image that the trading partners are organized to surround the customer, in contrast to the linear flow of trading partners in a traditional supply chain.

T

Technology infrastructure—All of a firm's hardware, networking, and software assets, including technologies that integrate applications across the firm such as middleware.

Tightly coupled information system—An information system that is integrated at multiple points and synchronized for optimum performance. Uncoupling a tightly coupled information system is difficult as the integration points are numerous and the systems may share common application code and databases.

Trading partners—All firms that interact directly with a firm to provide goods and services, including firms providing direct raw materials and firms providing distribution services.

Transaction system—Any system for processing the daily transactions that occur within a firm's functional areas, such as order entry, order fulfillment, and billing. These systems automate what would otherwise be labor-intensive and error-prone activities.

U

Up-selling—Persuading a customer to buy a product or service that is superior in attributes, and costs more, than the one under consideration. For example, if a customer wants to buy an off-the-rack suit but is persuaded by the salesclerk to buy a custom-made suit, up-selling has occurred.

Upstream firm—In the flow of goods and services along a traditional supply chain, a trading partner that supplies raw materials, components, and services to a downstream firm.

V

Value-add process—Any process within a firm that adds value to a product or service that is additional to the costs of materials, packaging, overhead, etc.

Vertical integration—All the functions that a firm performs in-house that are related to sourcing, making, and distributing the finished product. For example, if a firm has its own delivery trucks (as opposed to contracting through a freight carrier) or manufactures intermediate components (as opposed to buying them from third parties), we can say that the freight and component functions are vertically integrated within the firm.

Virtual enterprise (firm)—A virtual firm is an organization in which nearly all functions are integrated from other firms, which have specific sets of skills, with the help of information technology. Custom manufacturing, marketing, finance distribution, and other functions may be virtually integrated from outsourcers or other supply chain partners working together across geographical or organizational boundaries.

Virtual integration—Information technology–based integration of upstream and downstream activities within the supply chain. In contrast, with vertical integration a firm owns the upstream and downstream productive processes needed to source, produce, and deliver the final product.

Visible costs—In general, costs associated with various transaction-processing activities such as requisitioning, ordering, auditing, and invoice and payment processing.

W

Wide area network (WAN)—A communications network covering large geographical areas that uses data transmission lines, microwave satellites, or a combination of both to transmit signals.

Web technologies—Technologies designed to locate and provide access to data resources on computer systems based on differing proprietary and open standards through an easy-to-use interface. The computer systems can be within a firm, distributed across multiple firms, or on the public Internet.

X

XML—See *extensible markup language.*

Index

About the Authors

Ram Reddy is a senior consultant with the Cutter Consortium and president of Tactica Consulting Group. He provides technology and business strategy consulting services to Fortune 1000 firms. He is the former chief technologist for a Fortune 500 firm and CIO of a Tier-1 automotive supplier. Reddy has written numerous articles on business strategy and information technology issues for *Information Week* and *Intelligent Enterprise*.

Sabine Reddy, Ph.D., is an assistant professor of management at California State University at Long Beach. In her work, Dr. Reddy has examined the use of information technology for coordination in multinational firms. She is a member of the Academy of Management, Academy of International Business, and INFORMS.